The Making Of a Beautiful Woman

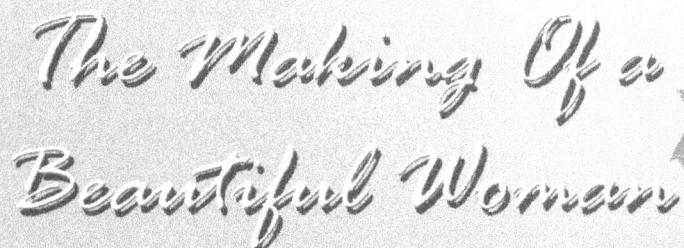

by Rosalyn A. Gillis

Illustration: by LeRoy Grayson

Publishing: by Jazzy Kitty Publications

The Making of a Beautiful Woman

"Beautiful Women are not Made Overnight.

Beautiful Women are Made Over Time…"

Rosalyn A. Gillis

The Making of a Beautiful Woman
By Roslyn A. Gillis

Cover Designed by Leroy Grayson
Published by Jazzy Kitty Publications
Logo Designed by Justin Ackerman
Editor: Anelda L. Attaway

© 2023 Roslyn A. Gillis
ISBN 978-1-954425-84-2
Library of Congress Control Number: 2023916997

ACKNOWLEDGMENTS

To my Lord and Savior, thank You for Your continual blessings over my life. You are my beginning and my end. You have worked my middle out consistently.

To my Bishop Steven Walker, you have been a part of making my journey beautiful.

To my brother, Pastor Whitney Blunden, my spiritual mentor and friend. Thank you, thank you, thank you; you made it easy for me to understand my walk with God.

Thank you to all my beautiful clients who supported Simply Beautiful & Co., whether you were there for a part or the whole journey. Thank you for trusting me with not only your outward beauty but trusting me with your secrets, problems, and your trials in your life. We got through them together; being your hairapist was a joy.

A special thank you to my sister/friend Sherray Gould McDonald, my very first client at 11 years old. It was nothing that she didn't let me try on her hair and she is still with me today; I love you immensely.

Chantal and Sharonda, my gifts from above, you both made me want to become the most beautiful woman in the world for you, inside and out. I hope I made you proud to call me Mom. No greater love than that of my children.

Lastly, my son, Sharif Hendricks, my son said to me one time, "Mom, you remind me of a rich woman." My son has seen the value of my worth without seeing my wealth. I love you three beyond this life.

I didn't realize that beauty was way more than skin deep until I grew up and started experiencing life. When I re-dedicated my life back to Christ in my late 20s and started reading God's word and learning the scriptures concerning my life as a woman, it propelled me to want to become not just a beautiful woman but a better woman, despite the hardships and trials, that I would face in life. Not knowing how these trials would break me make me feel ugly and unworthy of God's blessings. I knew I needed God's grace for my journey and for becoming the beautiful woman I wanted and needed to be. Join me as we journey down this path of becoming a beautiful woman together.

Becoming a beautiful woman don't happen overnight

Becoming a beautiful woman happens over time.

Enjoy!

DEDICATIONS

To all the important, beautiful women in my life.

First, my mom, Carolyn L. Gillis, and my daughters, Chantal C Hendricks, and Sharonda D. Hendricks.

My sisters, Chanda Mobley, Pamela Evans, and Diane Hill. These ladies all played a great part in my sisterhood with them. We cried, prayed, and supported each other through writing our books. God bless you, beautiful women of God.

TABLE OF CONTENTS

INTRODUCTION i

My Beginning 01

My Disobedience 03

My Gifts and Talents 04

The Dream Girl 06

My Best Life 07

The Change 09

The Crossroad 11

Leaving the Nest 13

My Life Now.. 16

Our New Life 20

His Fight 23

Re-Dedication 25

Our Protection 27

The Promise 38

My Covering 42

Going Through Anxiety 45

The Hardship.. 48

The Depression 52

The Hustle 57

My Turn 61

New Beginnings... 71

Taking My Life Back... 77

The Sacrifice 85

Where God Wants Me 93

Finding My Way 100

Take Flight 105

ABOUT THE AUTHOR 111

INTRODUCTION

Existence through my experience and God's words.

The Making of a Beautiful Woman was birthed from my full beauty salon, Simply Beautiful & Company. Being a hairstylist for over 32 years taught me a lot about being a woman. Not just beautiful on the outside but beautiful inside as well. Making women look beautiful on the outside was easy with all the different hairstyles, beauty, tips, make-up, jewelry, and clothing to top it off. However, convincing her to be beautiful on the inside well, was challenging because of all the trials and tribulations that can cause a girl to feel ugly on the inside and lack her self-esteem that she needs to feel beautiful.

I started incorporating some principles with every appointment. I made it my business to encourage every woman to be better inside than out, no matter what they were going through. I gave them God's word concerning us as women; I reassured them that God was the center of our beauty and that beauty was way more than skin deep.

MY BEGINNING

My journey as a hairstylist began when I was 11 years old; I was the youngest of three girls and one of the things that we got done regularly was our hair. My mom would wash our hair on Saturday, braid it in four big braids, and we would sit under the hooded dryer in turns. I went last because we had other chores to do before we could go outside. Once we were done with all that, she would press our hair and put these tiny curls in our hair that would last until the next time, approximately a month. So I would mess around with all different styles with my curls, all different up-dos, twists, and ponytails, and my friends would adore my styles. I started practicing on some of my dolls to perfect some of my styles. It wasn't long before some of my friends asked me to do them on their hair, so I did.

I remember my mom took ill and had to go into the hospital for a week or two and I asked, "Who is going to do our hair?"

She said, "I already have that worked out; all you girls have to do is wash your hair, put it in braids like I do and sit under the dryer."

And I always remember Ms. Ruth; she came early Saturday morning to do our hair. Sometimes, it would be just me because my sisters didn't want anyone but our mom to do their hair. Not me; I wanted my hair done. I didn't care who did it. I needed to look pretty all the time and my hair was a great part of my beauty as a young girl.

This young lady lived across the street from us; she always asked, "Roz, who did your hair? It really looks pretty."

I said, "Miss Ruth or my mom." Whoever was available to press and curl me did it, but I styled it.

And she asked, "Can you do my hair like yours?"

I said, "Yes," with all the practice on myself and my dolls, I was confident I could bring this style to light on someone else. And that began the start of me doing hair.

I started practicing all the updos that I did on my hair. I asked my mom if I could get some extra pins and rollers so I could be ready to do what people saw on me. I was confident in my style because that's all I did. After getting my hair done, I would stay in the mirror for hours doing different styles on my newly pressed hair. I loved being in my room because it felt like my own little apartment, and when I finally came out, I looked like I was going out to dinner or some date. My dad was always somewhere lurking.

He would say, "Where do you think you're going?"

Of course, I'd say, "Nowhere," because I had nowhere to go.

I just like looking like that. But those days soon ended because my big sister across the street asked if I could come over to her house to do her hair and my mom said yes, and that was my way out.

MY DISOBEDIENCE

So here I am, a little more skilled in doing hair and now I have a steady clientele in my neighborhood. I started braiding little girls' hair, then moved up to pressing and curling hair in my kitchen by age 13. My mom didn't allow me to do anyone's hair when she wasn't home to monitor me because pressing hair had to be done by a stove heat and you could burn someone's hair out. So I wasn't allowed to do it if she wasn't home, but of course, I would be defiant and do it anyway until I decided to press my little sister/friend Millicent's hair and dropped the straightening comb out of my hand on the side of her face. She had a burn mark on her face; boy, was I in trouble. So I wasn't allowed to press any more hair, just hairstyles that were already pressed or relaxed. I got bored and moved on to the next thing in my neighborhood; I started dancing.

MY GIFTS AND TALENTS

I went over to my neighbor's house, where we did some dancing. She was a ballet dancer, so she taught me how to do ballet. On the days I was there, her mom would ask me to scratch her scalp, oil it, and roll it up. So I asked my mom if I could start doing hair again. She said no, not in the house. So I made house calls, rolled hair, oiled their scalp, and styled them. So I was a busy little bee in my camp.

I would style my sister's friend's hair for their dates and other Friday special events. Then, I started playing with makeup. So, of course, I went to my mom and talked her into getting me some makeup. So she contacted someone she knew who could teach me how to put it on. So, I was introduced to Mary Kay makeup.

It was 1978, I was 14 years old and learning about the beauty world. My mom set up for the Mary Kay lady to come to our house and do a demonstration on me, my mom and one of my sisters. I was excited and couldn't believe my mom was down for this.

She said, "If you're going to do it, you're going to do it right."

"Yesss, Mom!" I loved my mom, for I was the only one of her daughters into all this prissy girl stuff.

So I went to school with my new look, hair on fleek, glowing skin, and lip gloss popping. And as long as I kept my grades up, I pretty much got what I wanted. But you know that it wasn't that easy because I was always in trouble. Mouth All Mighty, my mom called me and so did my teachers. Because I was always on punishment on the weekends, I got bored, so onto the next project. I had to think of something to do in the house with my hair done, my face looking good, clothes laid out and I couldn't enjoy the outside. So I remember watching TV and the commercial came on for kid models, Barbizon Modeling Agency, so I took down the number and you know what happened.

So here I am, confronting my mom with another one of my bright ideas. She said OK, but she needed to run it past my father and his thing was how much it would cost. Getting them to do that for me was challenging, so I went to my grandmother (Momma), my father's mother, who gave me the money. I began to do my homework on what modeling school I wanted to go to. Barbizon was out because of my age.

THE DREAM GIRL

So in 1981, I was accepted into the John Roberts Power Modeling and Charm School. I was so excited. I attended school on Saturdays in Center City. We learned everything except modeling in the beginning.

I was in a class with young girls from all over the city. We learned how to speak properly and hold our cups for sipping a glass of drinking water. Every Saturday, we learned something new and had to go home and practice for the next class. The next thing we learned was how to sit in a chair and how we should sit with our legs crossed or uncrossed. We learned how to stand properly, especially with heels on. We had to learn to use our facial expressions properly. We learned what outfits to wear for certain occasions, including business, work attire, party attire, and church attire, and we even learned what outfits to wear just to go to a movie. I learned so much in my first year about becoming a classy lady, even before I became one.

In my junior year, we finally started hitting the runway, learning how to walk in a fashion show. We had to bring in our shoes so we could be taught how to walk in them.

Our teacher was everything; she said, "It's all in the way you walk, all in the way you hold your head up and glide down the runway." I was in heaven, yall; learning all these things was truly a part of the young woman I wanted to become.

MY BEST LIFE

I was so into my life I really had it going on. Now, with a full weekend, my dad couldn't find anything extra for me to do. Saturday classes and Sunday church that was also a full day for me. I was on the choir, a junior usher, and on the church track team, so we practiced for everything at our church. While Rock Baptist Church was my foundation in my youth, hats off to my parents for rearing me up in church. I never forgot my spiritual background, for I knew I would need it throughout my life.

I headed to high school with a few things under my belt. I joined the cheerleading team. Of course, we had to try out, so I prepared all summer for that. So, when school started, I had to follow the routine they showed us and wait for the names to be called for those they chose. Yes, my name was called. Listen, yall, I was all in my glory that I started feeling myself; high school got hard. I started messing up royally, missing class. Just being in other stuff that I thought was more important than class. So you know what happened after that? I couldn't be on the cheerleading squad anymore until my grades improved. My parents weren't playing with me; I also had to put my modeling classes and activities on hold until I brought all my grades up. I got discouraged.

I worked hard until the end of the year. I was still short in a few classes and had to attend summer school. So, I went from the end of July until mid-August. I was so mad until I started meeting new people; that was just what I needed to get me back on track. I needed my parents to trust me again to regain some of my privileges. I got to enjoy the rest of the summer and just prepared for school. This time, I took my grades more seriously, settled down and got through my junior year with flying colors. Before you knew it, I was in 12th grade and so ready to graduate and move on to the next level.

Eighteen was looking good; I wasn't sure what I would do next. I wanted to go to college for fashion design, but my dad had one rule regarding his daughters: we had to be responsible for our own financial status for college. He feared we would start dating boys and forget about our education, so we had to pave our way. So I got a job and continued at John Robert Powers in the last year of my three-year course there. I worked and went on to become a senior model. I took different little jobs that came up for some local designers; I didn't get the real paying ones because of my height, but I still had fun enjoying the ride, swimming parties, and modeling swimwear. I got to do some of the girls' hairdos for some of the events we had to do. I was really enjoying my new life; we had an event every Saturday. I was barely home on the weekends; I still had to get permission. They said yes, as long as I was safe, my parents were good with it.

THE CHANGE

Then life happened, let's take a MOMENT OF SILENCE. My life took a big turnaround, not being responsible or taking care of what was important for my life at this age and stage. One month before my 19th birthday, four months before graduating from modeling school, I found out I was pregnant. Wow, couldn't imagine telling my parents this, especially my dad. I had so many plans for my birthday and now my life is not about me and what I want.

I discussed this with my boyfriend; he told me the decision was mine and that he would be fine with whatever I decided. He was already working as the manager at one of the fast-food franchises, so at least our child would be cared for. Now, the hard part is telling my parents mom first and then going from there.

So, I met with my mom first because she was easy to talk to; she was very disappointed in me. I felt really bad because she trusted me; she always had my back regarding my father. My father's military background caused him to raise us under a very strict and structured lifestyle without any fun. My mom brought the balance to our family; we escaped the torture thanks to her. My father was unhappy about me being pregnant, so he finally sat me down after weeks of not saying anything and said that once this baby was born, the father and I had to make our own home for our child. I was already scared to death about becoming a mom, let alone being on my own, raising a child. I knew I had to get my stuff in order at that point.

Life went on; things weren't the same around the house, except our chores still went on for me. Both parents worked, so I still had to make dinner for the family; no skipping out on your responsibilities. My dad made sure I understood that it doesn't matter what's going on; this is your job at home and as long as you're here, they will get done. Some days, I was just tired and didn't feel like doing housework, so I would go to my boyfriend's house to escape my father's rules. I wanted him to say that I didn't have to do chores anymore because of my situation, but I knew he wouldn't. Therefore I had to suck it up, return home, and deal with my mess. I made a grown-up decision to become a mom while I was under my father's roof, so I had to put my big girl panties on and put a plan in place for when the time came for me to move on, keep my head up, and continue going to my Saturday classes because I was close to finishing modeling school.

Things got a little rough, but I couldn't quit. My life was no longer about me. I stayed close to my mother because I knew I would need her support. My sister was a big help, too; she always looked out when she could. I was the last one at home, so she understood; she knew my dad was on my heels. I worked it out all day, trying to stay in my room or downstairs doing little stuff around the house. I sewed a lot; I learned how to make pillows in school; they no longer have those classes. I also knitted; I started a blanket but just couldn't seem to finish it. But I continued styling some hair and still had some of my dolls just to do hair on to keep up with the latest styles. I also had the latest Jet Magazine. I cut out the stylish pictures and put them on my wall to remind myself how I wanted to look. I loved the swimsuits the ladies wore. I always wish that I would be one of those models one day. But that was wishful thinking; I was always told I was too short for the runway.

THE CROSSROAD

W ell, the time has come for me to graduate from modeling and charm school. I kept my pregnancy a secret; nobody knew, not even my teacher, until the night of our big fashion show. A program for graduating night was a big fashion show award ceremony for all the girls that finished the three-year course. I was ready; it was bittersweet because everything I worked for and looked forward to was not like this. But I wasn't going to stop because of my condition.

My mom, sister and my friend came to the celebration. I pulled off wearing some of the outfits the designers brought for us girls to wear. When it was my time to go out on stage, I killed it and my family was right there cheering me on, everyone except my dad. I was a little sad because I wanted him to see that I still did what I had to do despite the mistake I made. But seeing my mom's face and her smiling at me made me feel better. As I strutted back towards the stage, my teacher winked her eye at me, letting me know I did a great job.

It was the grand finale; we all hit the runway with our names called and our certificates were given. When they got to me, my family stood up and clapped, which made me feel good and from there, I knew that I wouldn't let anything stop me, no matter what came in my life.

After the show was over, my instructor came to the dressing room and congratulated all the ladies and told us it was a joy, that we were her best class, and wanted to see us in the future on the runways of New York.

Upon leaving, she stopped me and said, "I'm very proud of you. I noticed the change in your body, and I watched how you continued to come, even when it got hard." I asked her did she knew and she said, "Yes, but I didn't want to say anything to you because I wanted you to finish without anyone getting in your way." And I did just that.

I was very proud of myself; that night gave me a lot to think about. I knew that I wouldn't be modeling anytime soon; I just focused on taking care of myself for the three months, preparing for the birth of my child. Being home now with nothing to do, I started reading up on delivering my baby and how to be a great mom. I went to different classes on Saturday at the hospital, and whenever they posted about new moms, I was there. My baby wasn't due until February, so I did what I could until I couldn't. My sister was my support person, so she went to every appointment with me because the father worked all the time and couldn't be there.

January came and things were getting tight; I couldn't get around like I used to. And early Sunday morning in 1985, my baby decided not to wait until February and graced our presence. A beautiful baby girl, I knew that I wanted to be the best mom for her, so I drew closer to God.

I prayed daily for me and my baby; I had someone to be responsible for now. I made sure that I was in the right standing with my parents because I knew I would need them. I got myself together and found myself a job.

LEAVING THE NEST

Her father and I decided to get a place for us to raise our baby. Be responsible parents for our parents to see that we are not just relying on them, so we did just that. It was hard because I had to get up really early. Take the baby to school, then get on the train for work. Motherhood was hard, but it was no turning back.

Two years have passed, our baby is growing, and so are we. We were only 21 and 22 years old, but my parents insisted we get married. It was against our family's religion to live with a man and not be married. So they sat us down and we agreed. My boyfriend proposed; we set the date and went from there.

Married now at 22 and pregnant with my second child. Working in the corporate world was not a part of my plans, but it was what happened. A long way from where I started and truly was different from where I wanted to be as far as my career. I don't see myself modeling anytime soon, but the crazy thing was that I still got called to do some modeling and said yes until I couldn't. The weekend was good. I was told about a modeling agency in my neck of the town; I hooked up with them and got started. It was definitely what I needed to boost back up my confidence. I like that I'm already married and getting ready for another child. I didn't know whether or not that was a good thing, but I'm here now. I participated in whatever I could until I started showing and couldn't model anymore. So then I just did something sitting, doing upper body, and some swimwear. It was fun, but I knew it wouldn't be long before that was over.

As my belly grew, I began having complications and had to be on bed rest, so that was the end of my fun. Home now for good until my baby comes. I just focused on being a wife and a mother. It was starting not to feel like a fairytale; I was happy because my baby needed my attention, and she prepared me for the next baby to come. I knew I would be a good mom because I watched my mom.

After months of bedrest, this little one decided to come a month early. Now the mother of two little girls, 3 ½ years apart. My mom had three girls; wow, what the heck was I thinking? Getting further and further away from my dreams of becoming a model, fashion/beauty consultant, and stylist. I just decided to focus on being a mom and wife.

Life got hard; my husband lost his job and I hadn't decided when I was going back to work. I needed to be home with my girls, especially the little one. My parents helped us out, of course, but my husband wasn't pleased, so he did what he had to do. Hustling was in his blood, so he took it to the streets, which seemed like all the Black men of our age were doing. I'm not a fan of it, but I guess people do what they gotta do for their families.

I'm a fighter, so I focused on myself and the children. There was no way I would let this situation get me down, even though it was killing me inside. So, after my youngest daughter reached an age where she could go to daycare, I searched for some daycares for her and some schools for me.

Once that was in place, our journey began as a student, mother, and somewhat of a wife. With pain in my heart, I took the leap of faith, not caring about the challenges I would face, but I knew deep inside that I had to fill the void.

Her father and I decided to get a place for us to raise our baby. Be responsible parents for our parents to see that we are not just relying on them, so we did just that. It was hard because I had to get up really early.

Take the baby to school, then get on the train for work. Motherhood was hard, but it was no turning back.

MY LIFE NOW

Cosmetology school was different, but it was a passion of mine, making women look beautiful. Being in school was good for me. I met so many different people; I loved it, and everyone loved me. The teachers loved my enthusiasm. I got along with most of the girls and the rest were haters. But I soon learned that a few haters are needed. They don't realize that they make you wanna be better.

I went through my beginners class with flying colors; studying, doing all the practice hairdos with our mannikins, and taking the book test was good, too. It was just hard studying when I got home because of my babies, but I was good once I put them to bed.

I went on to the junior class, and my life got harder. My homefront was ragged; nothing was good. My husband was out there; you name it, it was going on: money, woman, and jail. All this while I'm trying to get through school and raise our daughters. My nerves were bad every day, not knowing what could happen to him out there in those streets. But it didn't stop me; I went on to become a senior in hair school. Being a senior allowed you to do real people's hair. On the clinic floor, that's where you got your biggest grades from. This is where you get to show all you learned from the previous classes, and for some of us who already have some experience with doing hair already. The clients range from middle-aged to senior women. So, each day, we had new women; some became our regular clients until graduation. We were graded not just on how well we did their hair but also on how we interacted with them.

You know, that was a win-win for me. I established some wonderful relationships with my clients; they felt comfortable with me. They began to share some of their problems and gave me words of wisdom. My older ladies also encouraged me to continue to be the best. We exchange pictures of our children, our faith, some recipes, and some laughs. I learned so much from these ladies while in my senior class; it made the season of my life worth smiling.

I took all of what I learned as a student on my journey to becoming the best hairstylist I could be. I graduated with all the junk that was going on in my life, marriage on the rocks, but I kept moving, finding my place in the beauty world. I found jobs shampooing hair at local beauty salons. I was already good at that; I prepared the clients for the stylist. I got to watch how the senior stylists did hair. I watched every style they did and went home and practiced on my mannequins or one of my friends. I watched to see how many women they could do in an hour. All that stuff was important: how they interacted with their clients. All this was important to me because if you want to be the best, you must know everything to take with you when you get where you're going.

The fall came and it was time to take my state board exam, so I found my model, practiced, made my appointment, and went to do my test. We had two parts: you did the practical first with your client. Then, you returned in a month to do your written test of all you learned from the book. I took my model, practiced on her, and we were ready to go. I took us to the testing site. I prayed and then went in and set up my station as we were taught. I got my model draped properly; everything was graded from start to finish. The instructor walked around, watching and grading each haircut, sectioning, and roller set. Everything we learned in school we were graded on in a time frame. The clock was ticking. I stayed focused and remembered that I would make it no matter what. I stayed positive because I studied, practiced, and was present in class.

The test was over and we had to stop when the bell rang. The last part was how we finished, which included cleaning our combs, scissors, our stations and finishing up with my clients; we greeted our instructor and then left. I went back home, thanked my client and waited for my results.

I then moved on to get ready for my theory testing, which was in a few months. So I ran into my old hairdresser in passing. We talked about what I was doing and she asked me if I would come to work for her while waiting for my license. I said yes, just what I needed. With all that was going on in my life, I needed this; I needed God to move in my direction. I needed my girls to see me doing something else other than crying and being sad.

I started work that week and became her assistant. I shampooed her clients to prepare them for relaxers, colors and weaves, whatever she needed me to do before they sat in her chair. I cleaned the bathroom, mopped the floor, and cleaned the stations, all to make the shop look good; I did it. I did it like it was mine. I wanted to be the best at all that I did, even if it was for someone else.

I got close with the clients and the reps that would come in to bring our products. They offered classes, so I signed up for extra. I remember signing up for a hair-cutting class just to perfect my craft. I learned different techniques with different haircuts, became fierce with some scissors, and then signed up for hair coloring classes. I began to gain respect as a stylist in the world of hairstyling. Even my boss, to the point that when she would get overbooked, she would let me do her client. I got the overflow and I used that time to do my thing. I took my time to get to know the clients personally. I had to be a good listener, as well as a good stylist. I heard all their stories, some good, some sad, but more importantly, they showed me how to keep themselves together, even during their trials and tribulations. These women reminded me that no matter what you go through in this life, put God first and never give up. Look to God for your strength to be the best mother and wife you can be, even if they can't be that for you. God is the rewarder of those who trust in Him. Times got harder, but I tucked every word those ladies told me and took it on my journey because I knew I would need it. I continued working through that summer. Things really got bad and my husband and I decided to separate. It was best that we go our separate ways while he worked on some things and me to stay to take the other part of my test.

OUR NEW LIFE

Now, I'm on my own with my two girls, staying with my parents and working every day to care for myself and my girls. I wasn't feeling my best; it was hard. I was young and already going through hard times. I didn't feel like how I was making other women feel, but I continued on because I knew my girls needed their mother, so there was no giving up.

This was breaking me down. It started showing up, and my attitude was different. I started to get short with those around me, stopped smiling, and rushed to get things done to go home to curl up in a ball and cry. I did this for months and it became my daily routine until one of my ladies asked what was happening with me. So I shared my situation with her and she said to me, "Maybe you need to go to be with your husband; maybe it's time to join him."

The time away was good and the season is up. So I talked to him about me and the girls joining him in Virginia and he was excited about us coming. So I prepared my family and my boss for my big move. Of course, everyone was sad; my mother took it the worse because I'd never been away from my family before. It was hard for me, but I knew I had to put my big girl panties on and go get my life, so I did.

The day came when my husband came to Philly with friends to move us. I said goodbye to my family and friends. My mom left so she didn't have to say goodbye and for me and the girls to see her crying, but that night, she wished me well and said, "You will always have a home here." We hugged and I continued packing until morning. I transferred the girls' schools to Virginia and on our way to begin our new life.

We found a beautiful condo in Virginia Beach that we rented until we found a home for us. I stayed at home for a while until I learned my way around; I made a few friends to hang out with when I could. I found a babysitter for the girls for those times. I started living a normal life until I felt comfortable enough to let my guard down.

A few months passed and we found a home that was good for me and the girls to be comfortable in, a school nearby, and childcare for my baby girl to go to. Now, back to what I do, I found a salon to work at close to my children's schools. I worked, took all my skills, and built a clientele in Virginia. It was good; I worked amongst other women. I was the youngest stylist there, but I held my own. When I didn't have clients, I gave out flyers to all who walked by in the shopping center where the salon was located. My clientele were students from the area, colleges, and army and navy wives. I met a lot of interesting people of all races and ages. I heard many wild stories while building my clientele and focusing on my business.

My personal life was shaky and my marriage was still on the rocks. I started thinking about all the stuff that I heard from my girls that I do that's in college. I started thinking about my life, why I got married and had children at a young age, and why I didn't choose to go to college; all that weighed on me. The parties, the pledging, and hanging out with your peers. Oh well, I chose what I chose, and I was OK with that. I realize everyone's journey is not the same. Getting the prize is the goal and that's what's important in the end for everyone.

I continued my job and gained more clientele, so my days at the shop got longer and I spent less time at home with my girls. My husband was not having it because he had a whole other lifestyle going on. So he definitely couldn't be at home, so I shortened my days and stayed home to be with my girls. I went to the shop three times a week; being at home wasn't good. I have seen far too much of what I didn't want to see. I realized that I really wasn't in a marriage; I was just there to make my children happy.

HIS FIGHT

The street life was real, now in another state, the drugs, the women, and the late nights of hanging out. All of this I had to endure and I still had to play the wife and mother and keep my sanity while all of this goes on day in and day out. Thank God for the few friends I made to have somewhere to go and someone to talk to when it got rough.

We did some family stuff when we could. It wasn't easy being around someone who made you feel like crap, but I did it for the strength of my children. Some days were better than others.

I started to ask about visiting home, so every month or so, he would drive me home to spend time with my family. I was so happy when I knew I would be with my family and friends, even with the heartache that I was going through; just being home made it go away for the moment. I hated when it was time for me to return, but I knew that the time wasn't up; I had to finish the journey. So I endured all of it, and I do mean all of it. I cried more than I ever did. I didn't have anyone to turn to except a few, but I didn't feel like they understood what I was really going through.

I remember my husband opening a cheesesteak shop, now on another adventure. Nobody had the time for anything other than work and whatever he planned. The store was in the same shopping center that I worked in, so you know, I got to see way more than I wanted. Women, women, and more women after this man. More and more rumors, more and more late nights out, parties, and heartbreak for me. So I met a young lady and we became close. She watched my girls while I worked and I just began focusing on me and my children.

We met a man who came into the steak shop one day who did real estate and wanted to show us a house in another part of Virginia. So we accepted and went to see the house and I loved it. It was away from the steak shop and all the other nonsense that I didn't care to see every day. So we bought the house, I found another salon to work at, and I started feeling good again. Going home more often was good for me and the girls, too.

RE-DEDICATION

Our new home was great and the girls were happy. They loved their new schools and daycare. I was actually feeling better, as well. Out of sight, out of mind, they say. I remember visiting the steak shop one evening, and the man who sold us the house asked if I wanted to visit his church and I said yes. I told him that I would ask my husband to come with me, but I knew that that wasn't going to happen. So Sunday came, I got the girls up, packed the car, and headed down the road. We made our way to service. My friend was there, service was good. I ended up re-dedicating my life back to Christ. That day me and the girls went up and God received us. That was the beginning of my life being turned around. I went back home full of joy. I told my husband about our day. He was happy for us and glad I found something to do on Sundays.

So happy about my choice. I started going every Sunday, me and the girls. It became a part of my life. Now, it didn't change anything at home; it got worse. I was completely stressed out with my husband's lifestyle that I started expressing my dislike for the things he was doing and what it was doing to our family, but he insisted that all he was doing was for us. Sure didn't seem like it to me. I couldn't wrap my head around how being with different women, staying out all night, and getting locked up was good for your family. I felt lost; I prayed and cried, prayed and cried. No one knew the many tears I cried over this. I couldn't really call my mom and tell her everything I was going through because I didn't want her to worry about us. So, I started attending Friday night service because I got tired of hanging out myself. It wasn't the answer to my pain. It was just a temporary fix that soon stopped feeling good. So, I turned to the church that I went to join that Sunday and became a faithful member. I started staying after church, fellowshipping with the pastor and his wife. They embraced my girls and me and we ate dinner with them at their house. The pastor started calling on me to pray. I was feeling good in my new church home. I really was doing what I thought would change things around in my home once I did what I believed God wanted me to do, hoping it would change but it didn't. The pastor assured me to keep coming and believing, no matter what happens around me, so I did. The more I believed, the worse things got. The night out turned into a weekend out.

The street life was becoming a problem, not just for our home but for him as well. Jealousy doesn't just happen when you're doing something good; jealousy can happen as a result of you doing something that somebody else can't do or wants to do. When that happens, so does acting out. People will threaten your life, your family, and your business due to jealousy.

OUR PROTECTION

razy things started happening; I started feeling we weren't safe anymore, so my husband got us a Rockwell puppy. The girls fell in love. We called him Raw. Oh My God, it was like a gift from God; it kept the girls and me busy for a long while. Taking him for walks, training him, and doing various activities with him and the girls daily made the day and night go faster. I had very little time to think on the negative things that were going on in my life. Raw grew bigger and bigger and more protective over me and the girls. Not many people approached us when we were out because of his size. I never thought I would love this dog as much as I did, but I soon knew he was heaven-sent.

I was working so much and focusing on myself and my children that I started feeling really tired every day. I came home extremely tired; I just couldn't get myself together. I didn't have time to worry anymore about my situation; it was time to take a trip home. We had a special event that we were a part of, so we packed up the girls and headed home to Philly.

I wasn't feeling well the whole time I was home. I threw up the entire wedding. I couldn't even enjoy myself, so I returned to the hotel and called a friend to come to my room. She came by and we smoked some weed and laughed about a lot of stuff we had seen.

I started smoking weed in my mid-20s to help relieve the stress and anxiety that I was going through with my husband. I asked my husband if we could stay an extra day until Monday so I could go to the doctor to see about myself. Of course, he said no, he had to get back, so my girlfriend stayed an extra day so I could go to the doctor and we would ride back to Virginia together. She was good to me.

Well, we were in Virginia. She showed me around while I was there and helped me with my girls from time to time. She had some of the same values I grew up under and some beautiful parents, so she was cool with me.

Monday came and I made my emergency appointment. I got to the doctor's office and told her my body wasn't feeling good. My hair was thinning, my skin was blotchy, and everything was off, even my cycle. My energy was at its lowest, but I continued taking birth control.

So she said, "I couldn't find anything wrong other than stress; you're too young for menopause; you haven't missed your period, so I want you to start a multivitamin, get some rest and drink plenty of water." I was OK with that, so I headed home to see my family before we got on the road back to Virginia. A long 5-hour drive. I hated being on the bridge that led us into Virginia.

My mind was already in work mode; I knew what I had to deal with, so I prepared myself. Back home, back to work, and back to my drama. After a few days, I started feeling bad again, so I up my weed supply so I didn't have to feel any anxiety. I stayed medicated, doing my wife and mommy duties.

A month passed and I started feeling like crap again, with no energy and feeling sick to my stomach three times a day. So I called my girlfriend and asked her to take me to the clinic. I was too far from home to see my doctor, so we went to a clinic in VA as a walk-in. We waited for hours to be seen. Finally, my turn, I returned to the office, where the nurse was waiting to see me. I began to tell her my symptoms and she said we had to do some bloodwork and a urine test. I was a little worried because of the marijuana in my system, but what the heck, let's do it. So after giving them my urine, she said, "OK, no sign of pregnancy, let's get the blood work done."

So we did that and I waited in the waiting area for the doctor to review everything. Then finally, they called me back and told me my bloodwork said I was pregnant. I was like, "Can't be; I'm on birth control pills." Then she said, "That's why your urine test was incomplete."

I had to get an ultrasound, so I waited another hour for that test to be done before I could see the doctor. Everything was done at the clinic on the same day, which was good for me because I really didn't have the time or money to go to all these different clinics to have stuff done.

Finally, I was on the table getting my ultrasound and the nurse asked when was my last period. I told her I never missed my period; it was off due to stress, but I never missed it. She said, "OK because the ultrasound reveals you're about 12 ½ weeks pregnant." I was in total shock, but there was a problem. My cervix was thinning, which means I was going through the same thing I went through with previous pregnancies, which caused bed rest, possible plug, and early childbirth. Complications that I wasn't ready to deal with, with everything else I was going through. So I asked if it was too late to abort and she said it would be because the clinics only abort up to 14 weeks and you're already in the second trimester of your pregnancy.

I finished everything and went home sad because I didn't want to bring another child into my life. A life that's unhappy and distressed. So I cooked dinner, went and got my children from school, and waited until my husband came home to tell him the news. In the meantime, I called my mom and talked to her and as always, my mom heard the pain in my voice. She tried to console me, but I chose my path. It wasn't easy for me to show emotion because I didn't want my mother to worry about me. Because I knew and she knew it wasn't anything that could be done but finish out this course.

My husband came home after his day of shenanigans and I told him, and to my surprise, he wasn't upset. As a matter of fact, he was like, "It's your decision, but you're already too late to do anything about it."

So I asked, "Is this going to make things worse, or is it going to make changes in our life for the better?"

Well, I'm in my pregnancy mode and things weren't good. I started having complications; I was always weak and tired. Funny how I didn't have any morning sickness, but I was experiencing something else that caused me to go back and forth to the hospital. That's because my iron levels were low; I was experiencing fainting because of it. My husband was getting worried about me and we discussed going home so that I could be near my mother.

After 3 to 4 trips to the ER and my doctor appointments, I was put on bedrest because of the pressure that was put on my cervix. Due to the problems I had with my cervix, I couldn't walk without having labor pains.

Spring break came, and I used that time to go home with the girls. I needed my mother; I needed to rest without worrying about my girls, so home we went.

It was Easter break and the girls were so excited about going home to Mom-Mom's house. A neighborhood full of kids that they used to play with before we moved to Virginia. My kids ran up and down the block with the other children their age. They jumped rope, played tag, went to the corner store for candy, and danced on the porch. I loved seeing my girls happy. I kept all my sadness locked up so my girls would never feel what I felt in their lives. So innocent and full of love and life, I couldn't bear letting them feel unloved or unwanted like I felt.

Home felt good; Mom's cooking, love, and care for me were heaven-sent. There's nothing we like a mother's love. Being home was just what I needed; I got to rest and regroup before returning to Virginia and my misery. I was too young to be going through all this stuff, but I made the best of it because it was no turning back.

Back in Virginia, I wasn't feeling this anymore. Pregnant and in distress because the only thing I could do was tend to my girls. My condition wouldn't allow me to do anything else; just trying to make it to my due date, July 1, my father's birthday. That would be a joy, but things got heavy. As this baby grew, so did my problems. It was harder for me to carry this little one. I ended up back in the ER from contractions, still a long way off from my due date. My doctor set me up with another ultrasound to see how the baby grew so we could prepare for an early birth.

As I lay there waiting for the nurse to come in to do the ultrasound, I was thinking what girl name I would give this little one. She entered the room with a smile and said, "Good morning, let's see what's going on in there." So we began to talk about my children that I already have, their sex, and what I wanted this time. I told her girls ran in our family, so I don't know if I'm able to have a son. My mom had three girls, me being the youngest. So she looked at me and said, "Your baby is in position to be born and the legs are open. Would you like to know the sex?" I was skeptical at first, but she insisted that it was so clear and besides, she knew my feelings about having another girl. So she made it easy for me to see the sex of the baby and to my surprise, it was a boy. So filled with joy, I forgot all about my condition. I was so overwhelmed with joy that I hugged her and told her she didn't realize how this changed my life.

I went home smiling and couldn't wait to share the news with my husband; he, too, was excited. I couldn't wait to tell the girls they were about to have a little brother. I fixed a big dinner that took all day because being on my feet was challenging, but I made it through.

I baked cupcakes, and they asked, "Mommy, are we having company?"

I said, "Yes."

They asked, "Who?"

And I showed them the ultrasound picture and said, "Meet your baby brother."

They were so excited that they asked, "When was he coming?"

And I said, "Soon." This made them so so happy.

Two more months of school and things got harder and harder for me. I could barely walk due to the pressure and weight of the baby on my cervix. I explained to my husband that this was getting rough and that I couldn't do much for the girls any longer because I was constantly in pain. So my girlfriend would help out with the girls.

The heat turned up in the streets and the police were all over the drug dealers and unfortunately, it hit my home. Here we are again in an uncompromising situation and because of that, I had to uproot myself and my children and return back home to Philly. The girls and I knew that things weren't looking good. I picked up the girls and all of what we needed and headed home. I was in pain the whole ride, but my girlfriend got us there safe and sound. My mom thanked her, fed her, and made her feel at home until she left. The kids and I were happy because I knew what would happen if I stayed in Virginia. I was not home, but a week with five weeks left, my water broke. My mom said, "You're not ready," but God had another plan, so we went to the hospital.

The hospital, for me, was a resting spot. I was full of negative emotions and couldn't really focus on giving birth to my son. They took me to the maternity ward and prepared me to give birth. Not knowing how far along I was, I explained my situation to the nurse because most of my care was in Virginia, but they had my records from my previous births. I brought them up to speed so they knew what to expect and they prepared for my baby to go straight to the NICU Unit because of the early birth. Even though my girls were born early, I never had any real problems with them. In my second birth, my daughter had a low birth weight, but she was fine, so let's trust God that my son will be fine.

I got undressed and put on the monitor. They checked me, and yes, my baby was in position where he's been for the last seven months: only 4 centimeters dilated. Now, we play the waiting game; while waiting, I was made comfortable.

My mom left to get back home to the girls. I was alone with thoughts and what was going on on the homefront with the husband was overwhelming for me. Because I didn't know what the future held for my children and me. In my distress, I remember to look to God, who was my strength. It was truly hard to do. This was a long journey of the street life, infidelity, moving from house to house, city to city to remain faithful in a marriage I was in by myself.

Now here, giving birth to the greatest blessings that God could give us women. While by myself again, thinking to myself, *"When will this end? When will my headache be at ease? When will I live a normal life without fear and distractions of my husband's street life?"*

Doctors were in and out checking my baby's heart rate because as I lay there in distress, it caused my heart rate to climb, which made my baby uncomfortable. So they gave me a sedative to relax me while we played the waiting game called dilation.

I took advantage of the rest because I was truly tired, and not just from being withchild. I was tired of the roller coaster ride I'd been on for five years. Being married to the streets was not what I signed up for, but I remained because I had made a vow for better or for worse. I was in it, but I couldn't tell my heart which was 26 years old to stop loving a man that I had been loving since I was 15 years old. I felt like my life had no meaning. I felt like nothing because of what I allowed to stay in my life with no change, holding only love in my heart for a man who didn't keep his promise. But how could you when everyone around you didn't remind you of your commitment to your family? No accountability, no remorse, no care about anything. But what the world says is more important than anything that has sustained and that is money and power.

I saw something different in my life: a mother and father. A family unit that works together when things happen. In the home as a whole, there was no outside force that separated the family. Our village was tight, even in our neighborhood. Everyone's home was a father and mother unit home in order. Kids were in order; our tribe was sacred ground. This was what I kept reminding myself that was what my marriage and family should look like. But it didn't, which broke my heart because this is not what I signed up for. Not being married to the streets, raising my children in a drug-infested environment that I had to protect them from because their dad was all in.

Because that was how he felt, he needed to support his family with the life of dealing drugs. My life was not what my family felt good about. Always on edge because of the other stuff that came with it. Now, I'm getting ready to bring another child into this brokenness. I held on to my faith.

The day was ending and I haven't dilated anymore, not even in active labor. The pain was unbearable so it was gonna would be a long night. I came in at 6:30 a.m. on Tuesday, May 26, 1992. The night has passed and no baby. The nurses came in to talk to me about inducing my labor because my baby was not moving. He is in position but not coming down and because my water broke 24 hours ago, they are concerned about my baby's well-being. So I agreed, but I had a natural birth with my second child because it was too late and I delivered 10 minutes after getting to the hospital. So I asked what the plan was for an epidermal; they induced my labor and said, "It depends on how fast it goes," because I was already 5 cm. It was no choice but to get started and get this baby out of the oven. So they began to give me the Pitocin to induce my labor, and within 20 minutes, labor began, and Lord have mercy on my soul; the pain was unbearable.

My sister came just in time for me to tell her to get those nurses in here. I needed that anesthesiologist in this room ASAP, but of course, they said he was making his rounds. But I was in labor this time and couldn't bear the pain. I held onto the bed rail and began to call on Jesus. I knew it was no way I would make it without Him. As I began to cry out to the Lord, something was happening to my body that felt like I was dying. Blood was everywhere; my sister ran out to get the nurses.

They came in and said, "We will check her cervix," and to my surprise, my baby was moving down, and there was no time for an epidural. They begin to set up for the birth. I was crying out in agony because I knew there was no way I could push this baby out without any pain meds. The nurses assured me that it was too late and we had to get this baby out; it was crucial to his and my life. My sister stood by me and I told her I felt like I was dying; something was wrong.

She said, "I know, but you gotta push." The nurse made me sit up with all the pain.

"Rosalyn, you have to get this baby here. When we tell you to push, push with all you got."

I sat up and pushed until I had nothing left. My baby's head would come down and then go back up. They continued to encourage me to push, but the blood I was losing was causing me to become weaker and weaker. They had to call for another doctor to come in and assist with this delivery. The nurse put the oxygen mask on my face and told me to push with everything I got. I pushed, and when his head became visible again, they told me to keep pushing to get his head out and they got him the rest of the way. I passed out due to the exhaustion they were able to bring me around. The baby was born at 12:42 p.m. on Wednesday, May 27, 1992.

I noticed he wasn't crying; they took him over, cleaned him off, patted his feet, and still no crying. I was so exhausted, with blood all over me. My sister, the floor and I couldn't believe I was still alive because it looked like a massacre in this room. They called stat and other nurses came in and attended to my baby. My sister stood in front of me, so I couldn't see what was happening. I told her it felt like I was dying. Please don't let me die without seeing or hearing my baby cry.

They worked on him, putting tubes down his nose into his belly and putting an oxygen mask on him, and after 1/2 hour of working on him, a small faint cry came through. My heart rejoiced and with all that was left, I praised God. They let me hold him and told me that they had to take him because he still needed attention. I lifted him up to God as I had done with all of my babies. Giving them back to God and thanking Him for this blessing.

THE PROMISE

As I lay there with barely any strength, they took my baby to the NICU for observation and I asked my sister to follow them as they rolled him out. They told me that something ruptured and I needed special care at this moment. They left me there until they waited for the afterbirth to come down. I remained on oxygen as my blood pressure dropped. They continued to care for me. They didn't really know what was going on. Once they were able to get the afterbirth out, they put me in a room where I had around-the-clock care as I still continued to bleed.

In the room, still bleeding from my delivery, I hadn't seen my baby yet. I began to cry out to the Lord because I knew something was wrong and they couldn't seem to find the problem. Nurses in and out of my room, checking my pressure and my pulse constantly and checking the bleeding. After hours of care, my body calmed down and I could ask to see my baby. They told me that he still needed care and they would bring him to me after the doctors finished evaluating his status. So I waited patiently while resting and praying for the both of us.

A nurse came in and asked if I would breastfeed and I said yes.

So she said, "Great, my name is Carolyn; I will be helping you through this process."

I smiled and said, "That's my mother's name." So I felt like God had sent me an angel to look after me.

After long-awaited hours, my baby boy was doing good, and I could hold him. I was so in love with him; he was perfect; he was the promise. It didn't matter what I felt; this feeling trumped every ill feeling I had. This was the greatest gift God gave me: a son. I felt blessed. I kissed him from head to toe to his tiny little fingers.

My husband called me to say he was on his way. I told him he was here and he began to cry. I told him he wasn't doing good at first, but now he was doing fine. He asked if he had all his fingers and toes. I said yes; he was all that I imagined he would be. I knew he was happy to have a son. I also knew it was hard for him to get here because of his situation, but I knew he would find a way. He kept calling to tell me how far he was; it shouldn't be long. He couldn't wait to see his little fella and I couldn't wait for him to see him either.

My angel came in and got me started on breastfeeding him. It was so weird because I hadn't done this in four years, but it was my pleasure to nurse my baby boy. It felt like a whole new experience, but he stayed until he latched on. He latched on and began to nurse. It was a bonding feeling, but I noticed that every time he sucked, I felt blood pouring from my body and the feeling of weakness came upon me. So, I let the nurse know that something was wrong. They came in and checked it out. They let the doctors know and they kept watch.

The night was hard; I was getting weaker and weaker. At this point, I could no longer sit up to feed my baby. The bed was full of blood that was leaving my body. I was waiting to be transferred to ICU because my body wasn't responding to anything they did. I knew it was time for my baby to eat because I heard them bringing him down the hall. When they entered the room I said, "No! Take him back."

"Why?" the nurse asked.

"Because I have no strength to feed him I lying in a pool of blood. Can you get a doctor in here to tell me what's happening with my body?" They took my baby and left and said that they would have a doctor come in. While I lay there waiting to see a doctor my angel Carolyn brought my baby back to me. She said, "Don't stop breastfeeding because it has nothing to do with your body." Giving it one more try, my feeding nurse sat me up to feed my baby before they took me to ICU. The worst happened; I became unresponsive, but the funny thing is I couldn't respond, but I could hear all the nurses and the doctors running in the room to hook me up. While my body lay in a pool of blood, I could hear Carolyn saying, "I will call her family." She held my hand as they prepared to take me to the OR to stop the hemorrhaging. In and out of consciousness, I could hear them saying, "Roslyn, hang in there. Stay with us; your mother is on her way." Unfortunately, it was too late; they had to take me in to stop the bleeding and give me a blood transfusion. My blood count was down to four; I was taken in. Before I went completely out, I heard the anesthesiologist say, "Hang in there; there's a God for you. You should have been dead 24 hours ago." I remember asking for my baby.

I woke up in recovery in the ICU Unit. Barely awake, all I could see was my mom and sister talking to me, assuring me that I would be OK and the baby was doing good. It was crucial for the next hour, my body stopped releasing blood and my account was beginning to climb. I couldn't use my mom's blood because she didn't get there in time to give it to me, so they had to use plasma.

I made it through the night; I could be moved to a regular room and hold my baby. I was so nervous about breastfeeding because of what my body was doing while feeding him, but my angel assured me that the problem was corrected.

A tumor had ruptured during my delivery; they thought that the tumor that came out of my birth was my placenta but it wasn't; they mistakenly left the afterbirth in my body, which caused me to hemorrhage and become poisonous. But glory be to God; He had another plan for me. Most women that this happened to died while giving birth. My purpose wasn't clear, but I knew God don't make any mistakes. The doctors were in and out of my room, reminding me that I was a miracle. It was the breastfeeding that saved my life. Thank God for my angel Carolyn, who was persistent that I continue to breastfeed my baby.

I was kept an extra day in the hospital to make sure my body responded to the blood I was given. But unfortunately, I got toxemia and swelled up all over. Now, dealing with that, this would be a long recovery. But I didn't seem to care because I felt like I was living a hellish life, so whatever. My baby wasn't doing well because my breastmilk was contaminated by my blood being poisoned with my blood issue, so he had Jundice. He had to be put under a light daily until the levels went down.

I was released from the hospital in my mother's care. My mom had to care for my children, even my baby boy. I couldn't care for him then, but I believe God had a purpose for my life. After pushing my son out in the worst condition of my life, I knew I would make it. Because I believed, if nothing else, my life was in God's hands. And if He brought me through this, I couldn't make it the rest of the way. I just had to hold on and keep believing.

MY COVERING

Healing wasn't easy, but I got through it with the help of my family. My husband finally made it to us to meet his son. He shared some crucial information that could change the rest of our lives. We just have to live each day, one at a time. My fear was back, but I knew I would be OK because I was ready to get on with my life. I got another chance to live, so I couldn't care less about anything else. My girls and now a son to care for; it was about them and nothing else.

Once I was able to go back to Virginia, I packed up the rest of my stuff and said goodbye to my life in Virginia. My time there was up and my new life would begin back home where I knew I belonged. Of course, I had to take off from doing hair to care for myself and my baby. We stayed with my mom until my husband was able to come here.

I was healing well, my baby was doing well, and life was starting to feel good. I was so in love with this little fellow; he brought so much joy to my family. My mom and dad lost their firstborn son when he was a week old; after that, they had three girls. So God saw fit to give them two grandsons. My older sister had the first grandchild and the first grandson, and now my baby boy was the second, so they were in Heaven having these beautiful gifts in their lives.

My mom bonded with my son because I couldn't care for him due to my illness, so he thought she was his mom for a while until I could get up and be strengthened. She loved him so much; watching her with him was a joy. What a blessing! It was powerful and made me forget about all the hell I was going through

Months passed and my husband finally made the transition back to

Philly. We got an apartment, moved and began living a somewhat normal life. I was always on edge because of the lifestyle he chose to live and the path he decided to take. It was never a day without drama, but we got through it.

We made it to the holidays, our first Christmas with a new baby. I decided to have a big family gathering with my family and his if they chose to come. There was always tension between them and me because of the stuff that went on with him and his street life, women, and other stuff that broke our family into pieces. But I went on anyway to take it under the chin and keep moving. The dinner went well.

We made it through another new year. My baby was growing so nice; I felt like myself again. I always believed in giving people second chances even though he doesn't deserve it so I welcomed him back in because I believe in love and marriage. I wanted to return to doing hair so I decided to get back out there and found myself a salon to start back at. I didn't really care for the neighborhood, but I went and made it work. One of my family members watched my baby for me and I went to work. It felt good to be back in the salon. I worked five days a week building my clientele and meeting new women. The owner really took to me; she made sure that I had clients. She invested in me because of my talent and my personality. Everything was going well; I was focused because I wanted this. So, I put in the hours to get my clientele up so I could move to a better place to do my craft.

Time went on, I went to work and home, cooked dinner, and let my children play outside while I played with my baby boy. I waited for my husband to come home and we ate as a family. The kids watched TV until it was time for bed. They got their baths and then off to sleep they went and then it was mommy and daddy time. My husband and I always had a good sexual connection because of our attraction he had for me since we were teenagers, so he always loved being inside of me. Lovemaking was the highlight of our night; even though his appetite for others was a major part of the problem, he still seemed to love his bed the most, if you know what I mean.

Morning came and it was back to the grind, taking kids to school and off to work. He would take our oldest, who was six and went to the school closest to where he had to travel. I took my three-year-old and my baby boy, who was 10 months old to daycare.

I worked all week and when the weekend came, my husband decided to take a trip in the middle of March. Why, I don't know, I could only imagine. So he and his friend drove down on a Friday night and the weather was bad. It started snowing really badly.

GOING THROUGH ANXIETY

T he weatherman predicted blizzard storm conditions, and I was frantic about this man leaving us, but he said it was a business opportunity, so he went. The children and I were used to him being away on weekends for business, so he said, I did what I always do when he wasn't around. I did special things for the kids, like watching movies and making popcorn. I let them stay up and play in their bed. I made jewelry and played their favorite movie on the VCR. I always made the best of our time together. I never wanted them to feel like their home wasn't a happy place for them because of how my husband chose us to live.

He and his friend made it to Atlanta safely, but the weather was bad there also, so they didn't get to make that connection. So they were stuck there in the hotel until they could contact his people. We talked on the phone as he called daily to check on us. There wasn't much either of us could do because we were both stuck in the house. He was in the hotel until the storm passed, just like where I was in my life just couldn't get past some things to move on to the next level until we get past this phase in our lives. I know my husband was trying to transition from the streets to regular life, but it was hard. There was already some collateral damage, so there were some things that couldn't be repaired, but he tried to move on anyway.

March 1993 was a rough month. The weather was cold and full of storms, so we were definitely looking forward to spring. He made it back home safely but was unhappy about not being able to make his connection. So, back to the grind for both of us.

The job I was at was going well for a while. The neighborhood was rough and I saw some terrible things. A young girl was going to school and a group of kids jumped her. Somehow, someone had a fork that used to stab her and with the fighting, kicking and rumbling, the fork went through her temple, and she died on the scene. I was devastated; I couldn't believe that no one could stop this from happening.

Things were so bad around where the shop was located the owner started talking about moving and I thought to myself, *"Here we go."* So, as time went on, I eventually left because of the moving situation. I couldn't afford to wait to be a part of this transition, so I left early.

Home with the kids now, going to my mom's house every day for me and my baby boy because I no longer had a job. I just took him out of his daycare to be at home. It saved us money. Just us, the two little ones, stayed home until I found another job. It wasn't too bad being home. I was just OK having my own and the kids like being at my mom's house and on the block with the other kids playing all the games we enjoyed as kids. That was a joy for me, considering all the hell I went through and still going through. I must admit it was a little calm right now, no real street activity from the mister, but you know what they say about that: the calm before the storm. My Husband's job was coming along; one thing that I can say about Mr. is when he puts his hands on anything, he will make it work. He always puts his everything into whatever he decides to do. He knows how to work the work of the craft that he chose to get with.

We owned a steak shop in Virginia called Phillies Steak and Hoagies. It was lit; everybody from everywhere came to get a Phillies steak and hoagies. This man could do anything he put his mind to; that's what I loved about him. He managed different food chain franchises. He managed restaurants large and in charge, but his desire for the street money was where he was at, and he made that work as well, but it didn't want to work for him.

God answered my prayers. I was a praying woman and child who took it into my adult life because I believed in God. My parents had us in church as kids, but I read my Bible and prayed. I was taught by both grandparents, on my mother's and father's side, to trust in the Lord and to take everything to Him in prayer. So I did, even though things were crazy in my life at the time. The fact that God allowed me to live through my near-death experience with the birth of my son was a clear sign He was with me. So I had to say to myself, *"He, 'God,' didn't make the bad choices; we made the bad choices or chose the wrong path."* We do, but He watches over us so the devil can't have his way.

I was always thankful in my heart. The street life that we lived and I lived as a wife was scary and dangerous. The things I experienced being a wife to a street man were not rewarding at all. There were days of not knowing whether this man would be murdered on the street or just being beaten to the point of no recognition. The cops were always at my door looking for him, so I never got any peace living this life with him. I sheltered my children from it, so they didn't know the danger we were in, nor did they know why sometimes daddy wasn't home. They were too young to understand any of it and I kept it that way. My job as their mom was to keep them safe no matter what.

THE HARDSHIP

Time went on and spring was finally in full bloom. My baby boy was growing so nicely. April came and he was one month from a year old; wow, time waits for no one. I was planning a big birthday party for him. We lived across the road from a park filled with all the children's sliding boards and neat stuff. I was excited and happy that his dad was around to see him grow. He loved his baby boy and, of course, his girls too. My oldest was such a daddy's girl he took her to school every day at her request. He fell in love with her the moment she was born. The only one he got to see born, maybe that's it, or maybe she's his real true first love. I'm OK with that because he always said they are the reason he does what he do. But in Hindsight, what about the other stuff because the street life comes with other tags that can't be explained but seem a bit like lies to me? Never in the dark about anything. I always had to keep my head in the game because I never knew what and who was next. But I stay connected even through all the other shit. It was hard because I wasn't the woman he had around. It was always about business, lie after lie, betrayal after betrayal, even from his family, who never held him accountable for any wrongdoing. My marriage was a joke to them and everyone who knew us because of the infidelity. Enough about this; it takes me down a dark path of grief because I knew what I wanted out of a husband and this surely wasn't it. My heart was no longer in my body from all the heartache he caused, but it was quiet right now because the jail held his prize possession, and now no longer a threat to him and no longer a problem for me.

It was a good, quiet morning; he got up and did what he always did. He took our daughter to school while I slept with the younger ones. After a couple of hours, I got up, made breakfast, and got the little ones up for their bath.

It's so beautiful outside I'm making plans for the day. It was just beautiful; things were perfect between us. Many ugly things were still left in my heart, but I enjoyed the quietness. I got a phone call as I put the kids in the tub. The person asked for someone who was no longer around, so I hung up. Then they called back to ask for him and of course, I said he wasn't home at the time because he wasn't, so we hung up. I returned to the bathroom to get the kids out of the tub, got them out, and got in the shower. Right after showering, I heard a loud knock on the door. Boom, Boom, Boom! I jumped out of the shower and ran to the door. I looked through the door to see who it could be knocking like that.

I said, "Who is it?"

"It's the police! Open up, or we are going to kick the door in!"

"Give me a minute; I don't have any clothes on."

I ran back to the room and grabbed a towel and my babies. I ran back and opened the door. Guns were drawn and they said who they were looking for. I said he wasn't here; he took our daughter to school. My babies are scared to death and screaming. "I told them that they were scaring my children!" Then, they called for a female officer to assist me while interrogating me about his whereabouts. The female officer allowed me to enter the room to get dressed while she stood by until I was done. I was escorted back to the living room and they asked again, "Where is he?" And I told them the same thing.

After 20 minutes of this, I asked if I could call my mother to come get the children and they said not at the time they needed more information that

I didn't have. So it was a waiting game for Mr. to come home. Around a half an hour later, they raced outside and surrounded his car. He was pulled out and thrown to the ground. I was screaming frantically and called my mother. She got there quickly. The babies were screaming; we were all afraid, but I knew this scene quite well. But this time was different. I knew within myself that this was it. They placed them in the car; he looked at me and said I love you and I was in shock. We took the kids back into the apartment. I was crying, holding my babies close. My boy was screaming and my mom calmed us down while getting the things for us to go to her house. My mom was always there for me because she knew that this lifestyle would put me at risk for anything, so she was always there. We went to my mother's and called his family to inform them what took place and things went from there.

It was weeks later; I ran back and forth to the apartment because I was just too traumatized to be there. My baby, who was three, was frightened by all this; my boy was fine. He was 11 months old and didn't know what was happening. So my oldest daughter kept inquiring about her daddy, so we had to come up with something: such a daddy's girl. She wanted to know where her father was and when he was coming back. But I knew in my heart this was it; all the stuff finally caught up with him, so there was no coming back, at least right now.

After a few weeks had gone by waiting on his court date, being transferred around from Virginia to Philly and back again, his time of sentencing had come. Myself and his mother came; I brought the baby to look good for him, but it didn't save him. He was sentenced, looking at 25, to life. But God and all His grace and mercy and all the prayers for me and my family, the judge gave him 10 years. I was devastated, my life was forever changed. I had to face my children and tell them their father was incarcerated. This was truly not what I had planned for my life to be, but it's my journey now. So, I had to figure out what was next for me and my children. After things took a turn for the worse in my personal life. Here I am again, having to put my business on the back burner to take care of my personal stuff before anything else takes place.

After all that took place in my life, it caused me a great deal of functional depression. I wasn't happy and it started showing. I was trying to figure out how I was going to pay my rent after my husband and I were out of work. Running back and forth to court wasn't putting food on the table either.

THE DEPRESSION

My two little ones' birthdays were coming up and so was their dad's. But unfortunately, he won't be here to celebrate them or his. May was always busy because my middle girl's birthday was two days after her dad's, so we always celebrated them together, daddy and daughter. Now, my baby boy's birthday was in the same month, Memorial Day weekend. So, change of plans. I was sad that Mr. wouldn't be around to see his baby boy's first birthday, so I had to make it special. Therefore, we moved everything to my parent's house in their backyard. I invited all his family and mine. I did all the decorations in what he loved at the time: Ninja Turtles. He loved them, so I made it happen.

My baby girl turned four, and my baby boy turned one; everything was a success. Everyone had fun and took lots of pictures so I could share them with his father. OK, that's done now, back to real life.

I knew I couldn't enjoy my birthday with everything happening. But my play sister was able to take me out with her just to get things off my mind. My mom babysat for me as she always did. I always enjoyed myself when she and I hung out. But my mind truly wasn't in a good place.

Back to reality, I could no longer afford my living quarters, so I had to give up my apartment and move back home with my parents. I had to raise my three children by myself with their help, of course. Never say never. I thought I would never have to return home, but here I am. I made sure my parents understood that my children were my responsibility, not theirs. But it was OK for them to help me because I knew their father couldn't contribute anything from where he was. This was hard for me and my babies, but it would either make or break me. I decided after all the breakdowns and hell, I went through the mental challenges, losing jobs and getting new ones, going through in my mind, getting physically sick, not taking care of myself. I didn't feel like this roller coaster again. I tried my hardest to keep my head on straight, but I was ashamed of my situation. I stayed to myself and kept my children close. I didn't really feel like talking to anyone. I was always crying.

After a while of feeling like the lost ugly duckling, I broke down; I mean all the way down. I was in the shower when it happened. My mother called my big sister to come over. They got me out of the shower and got me into bed. I was lost; I couldn't even remember who I was anymore. This had gotten too much for me. My mom was so worried about me. She reminded me of all the times I prayed for better for everyone; now she said it's time to pray for yourself. And I did just that. I prayed that God would pick me up and turn my life around. I prayed that I would start believing in myself again.

After months of dealing with my trauma, I found a nice salon near my home to work at. One of my neighbors, who also just moved here from Virginia, had three girls watching my babies for me. So, I was on my way to feeling better about myself. I couldn't wait to start back to working on my craft. I still did a little hair on the side; I traveled to them to make some extra cash until my start date. I started coming outside on the porch with my family and talking more with my neighbors. I didn't want to be asked any questions about anything just wanted to watch my children play and have fun with the other kids. I didn't want them to feel any sadness, so I prayed with them every night before bed and they said a prayer for their dad. They always asked when he was coming home; no, something I wanted to talk about to them. They didn't need to know and I didn't want anything to impede their happiness.

My day came to start work, and I was super excited. I went in and spoke with the owner and his wife. I shared my experience with them and told them I could bring a lot to the business. They were excited for me to start. I explained that my hours must be respected Because of my childcare situation. I did that because they wanted to know the shift that would work best suit me, so I took the 11 to 7. It was Tuesday through Saturday. I came in on Monday to set up my station to prepare for my start date and got the children ready for my sister's friend to care for them; my parents were on just in case something went wrong or if she couldn't do it on some days. I was ready, so I thought. I was still dealing with anxiety and depression, so I kept telling myself I could do it. I just had to look up because He brought me this far.

I was ready to walk through the doors of the shop. It was Wednesday morning, 1994. I made it one year that Mr. has been gone, and now I realize that I am really out here on my own, taking care of my babies without his help or his presence in our home. *"I can do this,"* I said to myself. I was the fifth stylist added to the team of ladies. They embraced me and I embraced them. I tried not to show the chip on my shoulders. I knew I had to make my own way in the shop, so I got business cards and flyers made up. So, I got out and promoted my business when I'm not doing hair. The woman I did before I left Philly was excited that I was back home and working in a shop nearby. So they came and supported me, which was good because the other stylists saw my talent and hustle outside the shop when I didn't have clients. I was getting much respect from them, so now I feel I was a part of the team. I became more familiar with the ladies; we chatted about our downtime. I got to know them and they got to know me. We exchanged pictures of our children and shared a few life stories. But of course, I hated talking about my shit cause' everyone knew Mr. and how he was wanted in Philadelphia because of his drug life and the people he associated with. Therefore, it was hard for me to talk about my personal life. I believe they knew something was wrong with me; my sadness started seeping through my smile. It was hard at times to keep it together because even though God was with me, I felt like He left me out here all along. But I kept it together because that's all I ever knew how to do through all the stuff I went through in my marriage. Well, I've pushed through all my issues to make this money the right way and my hustle paid off. Now, I have a steady weekly clientele. I was happy as hell because I hated the feeling of being left out or left behind.

Life was starting to feel normal for us, but I hated when the weekend came. The prison visits weren't easy and made me feel degraded by the way they handled you through their processing system. Some of the guards always had to be extra with the pat down and I wasn't the friendliest person when I came there. I had been to four prisons before he finally came to Fort Dix, where he was finishing his time. So I was over the bull crap and the money thing me off these visits. But it was my life, so what the hell. Now I know to have the Lord, without a shadow of a doubt. But I had my own coping method, and God knew my struggle was marijuana.

I smoked what they called weed every single day to cope with my reality. And yes, it worked for me for the time, but I didn't let that get in my way of any of my work. I couldn't bring myself to take those pills that they wanted to give me for anxiety and depression. So I chose my own drug to cope with my shit. Yes, I said it, "My shit." I felt like my burdens were too heavy for me to carry. It wasn't an excuse to smoke, but a way out in my mind.

THE HUSTLE

Working at the shop was great. I got to know everyone in a good way. We did photo shoots, had lunches together, took breaks, and walked through the neighborhood. We had to give our flyers out; I was in my element. Now, things were going well, but I started noticing myself being in the shop past my last appointment, which was 7 p.m. If someone walked in after seven, I would put them in the waiting area for me when I clearly said I needed to respect my time. I did the client that came in after 7 while my other clients were under the dryer. So when I started that client and another walk-in, I added them, too. This became a major problem because instead of getting home at 8 o'clock, no later than 9:15. It was 10 or 11 o'clock, which was a no-no. The young lady in my children's care was on the clock from 10:30 a.m. until 3 p.m. My parents took them after that, so they definitely had a problem with that. So I spoke up about it to his wife, and of course, she passed the blame on her husband. So when I confronted him, his answer was they only wanted a wash and curl and I know how fast you can get that done. You know there was a glitch in every system. He wanted the extra money and I wanted to get home. Don't get me wrong, I respected his hustle, but it can't be me doing the hustling after my time is up. But of course, he kept slipping me these clients after hours and my parents started complaining about my late nights at the shop. They were reminding me of the fact that my children needed to be fed and in bed by a certain time. My father was always a father of order, so the same way he brought us up was the same requirements he wanted me to meet when it came to my children. Especially living in their home, rules were serious business in my parent's house. The hustle became real; this man liked my style, personality and charm. I knew how to dress up my pain and turn it on to who I believed I really was. That's what attracted people to me, so it was easy getting my clients, but my talent, personality, and professionalism kept them. My boss was intrigued by my talent for his own greed. It was good until it wasn't.

The winter was fast approaching, and I had to get a handle on my schedule because my children would soon start school and things would be different. It will be only me getting them up in the morning, breakfast, and off to school and my baby boy to childcare. So it wasn't possible for me to do any more late nights at the salon. I played my part, though, cause getting that bag was the goal: saving up to get my own place for me and my babies. I knew it wouldn't be easy, but I had a plan. So, I continued grinding the rest of the summer. Every morning, I clocked in and looked at the books to see how many clients I had for the day so I would know how to move. Of course, they didn't want you checking your books, especially me, because they knew I was starting to have a problem staying after my time was up. Therefore, they would have weekly meetings for us so they could express their gratitude and tell us what our job consisted of. But I had to let them know I got it, but I have children I got to get home to.

Time went on and nothing really changed because they were about the money. I wasn't mad about that. You know when you're single and don't have any responsibilities, then you can move how you want. But you must move differently when you're married, have children, a mortgage, a car note, and other bills. Everything, and I mean everything, was left on me. My parents were there just for support, not to take over and that was established from the door. So when I say I couldn't be in the salon past a certain hour, it wasn't because I didn't want to or even need the extra money; I couldn't because of my responsibilities at home. My parents instilled in us growing up to be responsible for ourselves when we were young because they both had jobs. When we got old enough to move around the house while they worked, we did. So cooking, cleaning, and making sure our house was in order was our job as teens. We didn't have outside jobs because our home was our job, and it was our responsibility to keep that up while they worked and made sure we had a roof over our heads, clothes on the back, and whatever else we needed as their children. So, we lacked nothing in our home because I had a father who made sure we were good.

Winter came, and I started coming in at about 11:15, which was late because my start time was 11 o'clock. I had to get my children off to school, so it became a real problem for me. So, my dream job was becoming a nightmare; the later I was, the later I had to stay, which now created a real problem. So I knew my time was about to be up.

The holidays came around and my clientele picked up. I was grateful because I wanted to give my children a nice Christmas. I grinded and asked my parents to be patient. I had to get someone to walk my children home from school and my dad would pick up my baby boy from childcare. This started wearing on me because I didn't have a break. Sundays were prison time with the husband; the kids were OK with going at first, but then they didn't like it as they got older. They hated seeing their dad unable to leave with them, but my strength was theirs. Trust me, behind closed doors, was my breakdown. I held it together for them; it wasn't easy, being young and all this on me. It was a struggle, but through all my tears, I kept going.

New Year's was approaching, and my parents made it clear that I couldn't work late, so when I went to the books, it wasn't on the desk for us to see our bookings. So I went to the manager and she showed me my schedule. They booked me way past the time I could stay, so I told them I could not stay past 8 p.m. because I didn't have a babysitter for the day. They said we would work something out. So I asked the other girls to take my clients and they couldn't, so I did the worse, I called out. It was wrong, but I didn't have anyone to watch my children, so I lost a lot of cash that day and unfortunately, it cost me my job. Yes, they fired me, so I went in after the holidays were over. They let me work the full day and handed me my last check. The owner was disappointed because of what I brought to the table, but my time was up.

MY TURN

I ran into my old hairdresser and employer from the shop I worked at before I moved to Virginia. She was my hairstylist as well. She told me that she got a building to rent a space for her salon, and she wanted to know if I would come to work for her. I said yes, so in the meantime, I did some hair at my parents in the shed that my mom and I turned into my one-chair space for me to do hair. It was convenient because I was home to deal with my children, but it wasn't what I wanted. However, I had to make it work until the shop was ready. We made it through the winter and spring. We kept in touch so that by June, the shop would be ready. I also was turning 30. Wow, look how much time has passed. Mr. has been gone now for two years with eight more to go. I looked forward to starting at the shop. This was a woman of faith and somehow, I knew God was in this move.

It was time to set up shop and I was truly ready. Doing hair at home has its perks because you must keep all your money. Also, you worked on your time and you didn't need a babysitter. But the downside was you had your private space in your home and it gets invaded, you are constantly cleaning hair up even after your clients leave and the kids never stop calling your name. So I was ready to get back in the salon, you bet I was, and there are other services I offered that I couldn't do in my home and they liked having that option.

The salon was very nice; we were located inside one of the apartment complexes in the Penn District in the center of the block and the other convenient stores. Therefore, we were right where the money was. We got to know our neighbors in the building. Most of them were students or older people who had been in the area for a long time and they supported our salon. We both could cut and style hair really well. I loved cutting hair; that was my favorite thing to do. Please, believe me, I can cut all races of men and women. Also, I was very sociable and it was wonderful to be in a salon setting.

Now, my boss was a Woman of Faith and most of her clientele were Christian women. Most older ladies in their 40s, some younger, were Apostolic Women of Faith. They wore no makeup, no jewelry, and they wore no pants. Most of them were married, so we all could relate to being wives. I was amazed that none of these ladies were offended by how my clients and I dressed or wore our jewelry. They understood what they believed and stood on concerning their attire in the Lord. I soon realized that our attire doesn't make us beautiful; real beauty comes from within. Wearing jewelry and makeup is optional because God decorates us on the inside. We just had to tap into the inner beauty that we all have as women. I continued to be me until the work of God be manifested into my life because I was dealing with a lot; I didn't feel pretty anymore; I was in my own way at the time.

I prepared my boss's clients for her until my clients came. I was good with that and enjoyed talking with some of the seasoned women. They spoke so much wisdom and it was food for the soul. I just listened to the questions that came.

I really didn't like people knowing my situation. It's just not something I wanted to share. Some people, not all, can be judgmental and look down on you when you don't fit the description of a good person, let alone a good woman. So, I kept my stuff tight and to myself until I could trust that I was in a safe space to talk about it. The life I'm living right now wasn't the life

I chose but was definitely a result of my union and connection to the man I married. Connections are important to who we join ourselves to in life. It is so very important, just something to think about. I truly believe that this move was set in motion long before I began this journey that I was about to be on. Being a hairstylist was my true calling.

My clients picked up and I was getting referrals left and right. I was pulling my weight around the shop. I was the shampoo girl when needed, the receptionist when needed, I ran errands, I cleaned, and wherever I was needed, I was there. I was grateful to be in the salon, so I treated it like my own. I made a name for myself around the area; the blessing was my hours fitted my life. I booked my own clients according to the times my children had to be at school. Here's the real blessing: if I needed one of the kids to come into the shop after school, it was OK.

My boss had three children just like me, so she understood the struggles of being a mommy. I didn't take advantage of that privilege. I just knew my three could sometimes be too much for my parents to watch. My oldest daughter wasn't a problem, my baby boy wasn't a problem, but my middle girl was a problem. I called her Dennis the Menace, a busy little bee. Thank God most of my clients were late afternoon and evening; some were morning people, but I spent most mornings preparing to shampoo my boss's clients. I was fine with that; I love chatting with her clients. They always had words of encouragement for me. I knew that was God; some of the things they shared with me were about being a Christian wife and mother. It caused me to take a look at myself in a good way. I wanted to do better and be better, not just for me but for my children and those around me. I wanted to make my family proud of me despite the road I chose to travel.

I continued growing in my new environment, really feeling good about being in the salon around the ladies. They always shared their faith in God when it came to their families. I went home every night thinking about all the conversations we had or me just hearing. I took a long look at my life, how I was living, and how I wanted to live a different life other than what I'm living now. I wanted my joy back; I wanted my happiness back. I hadn't been happy in a long time. I knew if I continued talking and sharing with the ladies, I believe I would start looking toward God for a better way of living that He wanted for me and my children, especially as a Christian woman.

I was wrapped up in my new job and forgot about my weekend prison visit. This became a problem for hubby; he started demanding our presence for a visit and started missing the kids. I swear going to this place was so depressing, and to be honest, I hated going and the girls didn't always want to go either. Saturday and Sunday was a full day for them. I kept them busy with dance classes, Girl Scouts, and other recreational stuff. I didn't want them to get consumed with our baggage, so me and my baby boy went.

I loaded up the car for our hour-long drive. I put on my music and made my way. I was grateful to have a car to go. My mom let me use her car to get around most of the time, but when she had stuff to do, we took the Greyhound bus, which I hated because they let you off on the side of the road and you had to walk up this long hill to get to the prison.

We arrived at the prison and had to go through a security system, and the guards had to pat you down after walking through the metal detectors. Once on the other side, you waited for your loved ones. Want to come out? Always excited to see us. He took the baby out of my arms and carried him to the seating area with tables, vending machines, and a playroom for the kids. I have this; it was a long 9 a.m. until 3 p.m. and he wanted us to stay all day. I would be exhausted when it was time to leave just from sitting and emotionally tired from this place. My baby boy always cried when it was time to go because he wanted his dad to leave, too. He held him close, kissed him, and reassured him that he would be home soon. My baby boy was too young to understand.

We returned to the car; I strapped him in his car seat and returned home. I would give him his cuppie and snack to keep him still so I could concentrate on the road and talk to God about this situation. I couldn't wait to get home and in the bed. I really wanted this nightmare to be over; it was wearing me down, and my new normal didn't seem normal anymore.

My dad would always come to the car, get my boy out of his car seat, and carry him into the house. My father hated that I was living this life with my children, but there was nothing he could do but step in to be the father figure my babies needed, especially my son. He needed a man's touch to guide him as he grew through his tender age. My baby boy loved his pop pop, and pop pop loved him. My father taking over when we got home was good for me; it gave me time to calm my nerves. My situation doesn't feel good right now, but it was what it was and I had to make the best of it for the sake of my children and my own sanity. Life can be challenging. I just felt it was being unfair to me.

I got the kids fed and ready for bed for school tomorrow. Monday was a holiday, so to speak, for barbers and beauticians. It was a day off for us to relax and do whatever. Of course, I used mine to wash my clothes, go to the supermarket, and prepare for my week. I couldn't wait to get back to work.

It was peaceful and talking to the ladies was the one thing I loved the most about being at work. They reminded me to keep my head up and have faith in God. Also, to remain faithful in your marriage to him. That is what helped me get through my troubles. I continued telling myself to keep believing that things would get better, so I continued on my journey.

The next Sunday came and I woke up to get ready, but my mom needed her car, so we took the bus downtown. My baby boy and I got on the Greyhound bus to the prison to visit hubby. We were dropped off at the beginning of the road; I picked my baby boy up because we would have never got there if he had walked. He was only two years old and still sleepy, so I climbed the long hill with him in one arm and my bag in the other. I sang songs and prayed to God until we reached the prison entrance.

We came in, I showed my ID and sat down until we had to go through the metal detectors. Now, the guards turned to pat me down. I couldn't stand some of those men guards; they took pleasure in touching some of us women. I never smiled; they said that I was evil and nasty. "Oh well, I'm not here to be your friend; just escort me to the waiting area."

Hubby came out and took the boy from me. We sat, ate, and discussed the kids and my new job. I told him how well things were going and how the ladies uplifted me when I did their hair. I told him my life was changing because of their prayers and encouragement. It didn't remove the heartache I was dealing with, but it made it easier for me to deal with it. The words gave me hope that things would get better; I just had to keep moving and hanging there. Our visit was up, we said our goodbyes and my boy cried as usual.

We left and headed back down the hill to the bus stop. I held him close and sang songs in his ear to calm him down. I prayed over my baby boy and promised him that life would get better for us soon, and I never wanted to see him in this place. He held onto my neck as I carried him to the bus home. He laid across my lap all the way home. I know my boy didn't understand what I was saying to him, but I was speaking life to his little soul like I did with my girls. I wanted every time I got the chance to speak of God's blessings I did, even if they didn't get it at that time. My children were all I had, so I chose to keep God at the center of our universe. I had to keep them together, no matter how heavy the burden was. Raising three kids alone wasn't easy, but thank God for my parents. There were times I would cry out to God, asking Him why. Why am I going through this? I'm too young to be dealing with this stuff. I hated feeling this way. It made me feel ugly inside and out, and it showed.

Sometimes, I would leave home early to start my day at the salon just to walk and talk to God with no smile on my face. I wanted the world to know how angry I was that I was going through this. Men would say hello, and I literally growled at them or gave them the evil eye. They be like, "Damn, Sis, who hurt you? You too beautiful to be that mean." I didn't like compliments; they were hard for me to digest. I didn't feel like anything of what they saw. I wouldn't say good morning sometimes to my neighbor; totally out of order. I wasn't raised like that. I was angry and unhappy, and it showed. But once I hit the shop, I switched gears, and my ladies were glad to see me. They loved how I took care of them. They loved how I shampooed their hair and prepared them for my boss.

The morning was my downtime at the shop, so I would sit in on some conversations and listen to them talk about the church and their services. I hadn't been in church since I left Virginia. I tried to visit some churches but didn't like them for me and my children. I visited the church that I grew up in some months back, but it wasn't the same. I realized that I had outgrown that setting. The church I joined in Virginia was totally different from the Baptist church I grew up in, so I just didn't go anymore.

One of my cousins heard I was back home and we talked. I told her I was in Philly for good and was working at a nearby salon, so she came by for a visit. She loved the shop. I introduced her to my boss, and we all chatted. She told us about her experience attending the Dudley Cosmetology School in North Carolina. Dudley's was one of the top brands in the mid-80s through the 1990s. Everybody building up their salon had all the Dudley products and attended their classes, so yes, we were impressed with that. We talked about our children; our youngest children, who happened to be boys, shared the same birthday, which was dope.

Winnie, she called me, which was my nickname that my dad gave me as a little girl and the only people in my family called me that. Others know me, and now my nieces and nephews call me Aunt Peach. Winnie, she said and asked, "You been to church since you been home?" I told her yes, but I wasn't too crazy about it. She said, "You should come to my church. We just started it and it's not full yet. We have prayer and Bible study at my house on Wednesdays and Sunday service at the Wynne Ballroom." I laughed because my sister and I used to attend parties there growing up with some of the neighborhood kids. Boy, did we have a ball going; it was one of those Saturdays that our parents from the block we lived on would say if certain neighbors were going yall can go and if so and so, dad is taking yall and picking yall up yall can go. Our parents were very different back then.

Boss Lady was very impressed with my cousin and our conversation, so she asked her if she would like to come and work with us, and she said yes. I was so excited for her to become a part of the salon. We always had a good time when we got together.

A week later, she started and I got to see her skills and she got to see ours. We made a great team; she likes to clean like me, so my boss never had that problem in the shop. We kept things tight, we ate lunch together and she learned some things from us as we learned some things from her. When we didn't have clients, we did each other's hair.

So, one Wednesday from work, I took her home and stayed for Bible study and prayer. It was similar to my church in Virginia. Then, on Sunday, my children and I attended the church, and they welcomed me and my babies. After service, they had a kitchen where they served food, so we stayed and ate and the kids got to know the other children. I mingled a little, a little hesitant at first because of my situation, but I'll see what happens. I continued going to Bible study and church. My mom thought that it was good for me. She didn't like seeing me sad and depressed all the time. But I continued. I would cry on some Sundays because that was the day I visited hubby, but I wanted me and the kids to attend church. The kids enjoyed going and being with the other kids. I felt good going because it was breaking something in me; not sure yet what I was feeling, but it was a sense of peace in my spirit. We continued from there, and the children bonded with some of the kids there, so they definitely liked going there, and that alone made me happy because they didn't deserve or ask for the hand that was dealt to them. But I made their situation as sweet as I could possibly do for them. I always told them that children are gifts from God and that they were my gifts, and they needed to know that, no matter what we are facing right now, you are important. I showered them with love and affection, and so did my parents. Especially, my mom, she loves all of her grands and it showed in every way possible. I so appreciate them for that; I was blessed to have them in my life.

NEW BEGINNINGS

Now, after months of attending church, we finally became members of Abundant Life Healing Fellowship Church under the leadership of Pastor Steven Walker. We were in church most of the time now. The kids were OK with Wednesday night prayer and Bible study, Sunday morning service, and then again on Sunday evening. They joined the children's dance ministry and the children's choir. I also joined the dance ministry for adults and later the choir. It's so good to be a part of something great.

I started feeling the feeling of being alive again. I truly had something to look forward to every week. I stopped looking at where I was and started looking at where I could be. Endless possibilities for my babies and me.

As I continued to walk with God, my relationship with Him grew. He started showing me things about myself and how He can change my life around for the good. My mindset shifted from feeling like a woman who was left to die to feeling like a woman God was with. I felt my life had a purpose, even with everything on my plate.

I couldn't wait to return to the salon and talk with my clients and the other ladies. I felt like I now had a story to tell about my God and church. I was a part of something. I knew it deep down in my soul, but I just couldn't say it. We chatted about our services and how the Spirit of God moved. It was an amazing thing that God was doing in me and my children. I still had struggles and shortcomings that I couldn't share at the time. I knew I had to pray about those things in private with God. I tried hard to never let my stuff hang out. I tried to keep it together for myself and my children. The closer I got to God, the harder it seemed to get. I thought things would get better and change would happen instantly once I returned to church. There was a process that I had to go through that they don't tell you about. But why did I think that anyway? My father always told us about consequences for every action; there's a reaction. Again, my life resulted from the lifestyle my hubby chose. I guess if it weren't this, it would be something else. I pressed my way on despite what was done that I couldn't change. Some days with tears, some days with a smile.

I got counseling from my pastor from time to time. I needed it. He assured me that God sees and knows all about my situation and to keep my head up. I felt better after counseling with the pastor; it helped me take this walk a little easier. I read my Bible frequently to help me with my struggles; it gave me a different perspective on things. There were definitely signs of change in my life. I believed the words I was reading in my Bible, which caused me to believe in myself again. When you have seen yourself one way in a negative light for so long, it may take some time to see yourself in a more positive light. But you will come through your trial through prayer and affirmations, confirming yourself, and standing on God's Word. Romans 12:2-3 says, *"And be not conformed to this world, but be ye transformed by the renewing of your mind that you may prove what is that good and acceptable and perfect will of God."* This was one of my scriptures that helped me through times when the devil wanted to mess with my head and tell me I wouldn't make it. If you are a woman who already suffers from low self-esteem, it won't be hard for him to remind you of your failures. I continued working on myself through counseling, attending positive things, and being around other women who have been through things like me and made it to the other side.

I continued working at the salon, saving money and building up my clientele. We hired more stylists and grew. I learned so much in this place; that's when I knew my time was up. I soon came to realize that some places are seasonal. God met in that place; I met those women because I needed what they had to help me to my next level. I went on to work at other salons on my mission to save money to get a place with me and my children. I took what I learned from those seasoned Women of God, packed it in my bag to use when I needed it, and shared it with other women I came in contact with who were going through rough times in their lives. Now, I can help them by speaking life the way God allowed it to be spoken of over me through the ladies that He allowed me to meet on this journey called life.

I continued raising my children in the House of God and they continued to grow. They were growing up so fast, especially the girls, and it was definitely time for them to have their own space. Therefore, I was comfortable now looking for apartments. I knew my budget and what I could afford, so I knew it would be challenging. My husband's time was four years away, so I wanted to settle in by the time he came home. So, in between shops, I focused on getting the children ready for school, their dance classes, camp, and the Boys and Girls Club. All these things I put them in allowed me to work and keep myself sane through all these motherly things I had to do. My mother was truly a big help, but she also knew that we had outgrown this space, and things were starting to get crazy around the house. My dad was growing weird with the kids being all over the place when I was working. So, I took a break from the salon atmosphere to focus on them. My parents had a vacation home in Montego Bay, Jamaica, where they spent their time away from Philadelphia when they could. They would buy barrels and pack them with all the food, perishables, clothes, toiletries, and other goodies for them and some of their neighbors in Jamaica. My mom was such a given person; I get that from her. I will give the shirt off my back if someone needs it because that's how my mother was.

While my parents were prepared to go to their vacation home, this was my time to show God that I could care for my parent's house as if it were my own. I paid the bills, kept up all the cleaning, and kept things in order. Mind you, I never lived on my own. I went from being a teenager to becoming a wife, so this would be the first time living in a house by myself and my babies. So, while they were still young, I taught them how to clean and how to do shifts around the house so they would know how to keep the area clean for when we moved. They understood that if they didn't do their chores, they couldn't go outside or play any games on the TV until they were done.

We ate dinner together and at a certain time and we talked about a lot. I talked about the Lord and how He blessed us during that time. I needed my children to understand why I believed in God and why I needed them to believe in Him, too. Because they're going to grow up and start their own families or maybe just go to college and be on their own. I needed them to know God for themselves and to take Him with them into their own individual lies. That's what we talked about at the dinner table, the goodness of God and how it was by His grace that we have food on the table and a roof over our heads. I wanted them to be thankful to Him for His blessings.

Times got really hard for me when my parents left for Jamaica; I wouldn't have the physical help, so I took a break from the salon. I needed to be at home for my babies, plus I didn't have anyone to watch my children while I worked. So again, I had to step away from the salon for a minute to get myself together. I had no one to depend on in my life but my parents, so while they were on vacation for nine months, I was pretty much on my own.

Making money doing hair was easy, so I did the traveling hairstylist thing. I took my middle girl with me, and my oldest took care of my baby boy while I went and made this money to put food on the table for my children. I was OK with wearing my big girl panties. I loved being a mom and running the house. I held it down while my parents were away; they knew that, too. They never had to worry about their home or anything while under my care. That made me feel good that my parents could depend on me. So I wasn't going to let them down. I continued traveling and doing hair for the rest of the summer until my parents returned home. They always left in January and stayed in Jamaica until August, so it was still hot here in the States when they returned.

Me and my mom were close, so we did everything together, especially shopping. So, while we were shopping down 69th St., we walked around to different stores and passed this salon, so I told her, "School was about to start and my baby boy was ready to go to school." I asked her if she was OK with me returning to the salon again. I really miss being behind the chair and talking with the ladies. Even though I had a lot going on in my head, I still was a friendly person with a big personality. My mom said yes, so I went in and filled out the application and trusted God for the rest.

A week later, I got a call to work at the salon I applied for just in time for school. I was so excited my baby boy was going to kindergarten. I was so excited for him; my dad was his buddy, so I already knew who would pick him up when I couldn't. The girls would walk home with the other children and their mom. The school was around the corner from where I grew up. Bryant Elementary School. I couldn't believe that now my children would be attending there. My girls were in Christian schools and the baby boy is now in a public school. Let's see how this is going to work out. I prepared them for the rest of the summer days to start school, and they were excited to start the new school and their journey.

TAKING MY LIFE BACK

Now, a stylist at my new salon and the kids are all settled in their new schools; now let's see where this road will lead us. This salon was different from other shops I worked at. I really had to pull my weight around here. These girls were fighting for the same thing I was. A clientele! There were days of sitting with new clients. I depended on walk-ins until my regular ladies arrived on their appointment days. But it wasn't that easy because no one wanted to pass off clients to me. I guess because the new girl only got the clients they didn't want. It was cool, though, because I needed the money, so I did them, even the most difficult ones. I did and they were amazed at how I communicated with those ladies. I remembered how to deal with my new situation. It was survival of the fetish.

As time went on, the ladies got to know me a little better, so they let their hair down, so to speak. They saw that I wasn't about any nonsense. I really didn't have time to be in nonsense. I had to make my money at a certain time to get out of there at a certain time to be home for my children. I didn't want to put that on my parents again. So I went from sitting in my chair, waiting on the walk-ins, to sitting up front so that I took them when one came in if they weren't scheduled for someone. I know that was a problem for the other ladies, but I had to get this money without steppin' on any toes. Therefore, when it was brought to my attention that I couldn't do that, I asked why. The manager said we had to take turns, which was bullshit because I saw her take all the walk-ins. She used the shampoo girl to greet them and that's how she got them. It was cool because I made up my flyers and took my walks. I've been down this road before; I know how to go fishing. I put my name at the top of my flyer or business card so when they came in, it wasn't no mistake who they wanted. I had to get some respect in that place.

So things were going OK in the shop; I now see how this goes. I kept busy and when I didn't have a client, I went outside. I wasn't for any bull crap; I already had enough to deal with. I didn't want any more craziness on my plate, definitely not in my place of business. I remained professional at all times.

Seven o'clock was closing, so I left if I didn't have anyone. My dad always picked me up from work with my baby boy. Seeing his cute little face waiting for me to get in the car was a joy. I got in and sat in the back so I could hug and kiss on him. I just loved my baby boy and he loved his mommy. All in my head about my situation, looking at my baby always makes me feel grateful, remembering how we both were at death's door during my delivery with him. So I never forgot that and never will. I always asked God why He didn't let me die. I felt like He knew my children needed me, so even though this was difficult for me, I made sure I tried to be better, if not for me, then for them.

The weekend came and I worked on Saturday, which was the hardest day for me. It was hard because I knew my parents needed a break from my children. Therefore, I couldn't stay all day. I had to leave at 3 o'clock and I made no money that day. I hustled more on my next business day, which was Tuesday. Sunday's was either church or the prison. I really preferred church because I hated going to prison, but my husband needed to see the kids and me. It made his day and it kept him close to his children. He didn't want them to forget that they had a father, which made him feel special.

However, they were getting tired of going because they liked their weekend activities and playing with their friends. So if they didn't want to go, I didn't force them; I just went with my little man. When I was tired from working, I wouldn't drive; I just rode the bus to get some rest until we got there.

Up the road we went; I carried my boy in my arms while he was still sleeping. He was getting too big for me to carry after a while, and he knew it was too much for me. So he walked on the rest of the visit and we sang songs. I prayed over him and repeatedly told him how it would break Mommy's heart if he ended up in this place. He didn't understand because he was just too young. I knew one day he would know the truth. But for now, I had to explain it as he could understand, and that was that Daddy was in that place because of something he did wrong and that when his punishment was up, he would come home. It didn't lessen the pain; my baby still cried after every visit. He wanted his dad to leave with us.

Back down the road, exhausted physically and mentally. I carried my boy and he was heavy. All I needed to do was comfort and tell him in his ear that things would be alright; tears rolled down my face. I hurt for my babies; they needed their father. I didn't grow up without my daddy and couldn't imagine it, so I knew what they felt. I had to give them the extra love they needed so that they didn't feel less.

I continued my journey; this hair salon wasn't the best. I wasn't making any real money, but I made it work until I could do better. The kids continued to go to school and made it through the holidays. I always made their Christmas big with the help of my parents. So they got lots of gifts and toys.

January came and it was time for my parents to leave again. This time, my sister came to live with us while my parents were away, so I had a babysitter. I worked and continued going to church and the prison. I was grinding and saving money so we could move by next year. But the worst happened: in mid-March, a blizzard hit, and I mean a big one. It shut everything down; no one could leave their houses because of how high the snow had gotten. Thank God we had food in the house. My mom always kept the deep freezer full in case of an emergency. And there it was, me, my sister and her son weathering the storm. We stayed warm and kept the kids together until we could return to normal life. It was a fun time; the kids loved playing in all that snow. It really wasn't anywhere to put the snow, so there was no shoveling; just cleaning your cars off, that's it. You couldn't even get out of your block. All the men of the block got together to make a pathway so at least they could walk on the sidewalk and the street; imagine that.

April came still some snow, but it came back to life again. It was back to school for the kids and back to work for me. I continued at the shop until May. We went to work one day and it was closed when we got to the door. No word from the owner saying anything. My manager called and she said that she couldn't reopen the shop. At the owner's request, we had to return later in the week to get our stuff. So we were all devastated. We had bills to pay, so two girls and I rode down 69th St., looking for another salon to take us in and get us a chair. We came together because it was crucial. This was our only income, so finding us a shop quickly was a must.

Later in the week, we got our stuff, and by the grace of God, we found a shop for two stylists and our shampoo girl; we were in. It was a big shop with a lot of stylists, an eight-chair salon with stylists on each side right across the street from the train station. Therefore, it was always busy and they made sure we had clients. We didn't have to fight for any clients. That was great because I was always busy and my sister didn't mind watching the kids. So I made that money while I could.

I needed to move soon; my children were getting bigger, and we were outgrowing the space that we were in. I worked all through the summer with no problem. I continued my spiritual journey and went to the prison when I could. It was getting tough because the kids had events I had to attend. So he wasn't happy about that, but the timing wasn't good. I couldn't neglect them; they needed me there to support them and I wouldn't let them down.

I worked all through the summer. I can't believe how time was flying. September came and my parents were coming back home soon. However, only my dad returned; my mom wanted to stay a little longer. My baby boy is going to first grade and I was so excited for him. Of course, he didn't want to go, but my middle daughter was in fifth grade, so she would watch out for her baby brother. As easy as that sounded, it didn't go that way. Every day, my sister called my job to tell me about in the classroom he was in had a problem child in it, so it was always some drama. I went up there before work and of course, a little boy with some special issue would get violent with some of the children. They couldn't control him and they basically did nothing. My sister has been working for the school district for a while now, so she was able to keep me informed.

I was doing really well at the shop, making good money. I really didn't want anything interfering with making my money, but it was too good to be true. This situation got really bad with the little boy in my son's class, and nothing was being done. He threw a chair at the teacher, and she got hurt really badly and didn't return. Therefore, there was substitute after substitute with no permanent teacher for his class. That meant that that child was running wild in the classroom and nothing was being done.

I spoke to my manager at the salon and told her I needed to change my hours and she was OK with it. So I sat in on my son's class time every morning until they got a new teacher or until they moved this kid out of the class to where they could handle him. The stuff I witnessed with this child was unbelievable. There was no way I was leaving my baby boy alone with this child in this classroom. He was getting up and going around the class, just hitting other children and let's be clear, he knew not to come near me or mines. They could not keep a teacher in this class because of this child's behavior. So here I am in another situation that keeps me from being in the salon, but I did not want my son's first-grade experience to be bad. Therefore, I did what I had to do. I went with my son to school every morning and sat in his class until 2:45. Then I grabbed my daughter and walked them home; I went to the salon afterward. This affected my money but I made up for it on the weekends. I went on with this until summer came. I was exhausted with this stuff.

I was so faithful in that classroom with those kids and all the substitute teachers that they asked me if I would return next year to work in the lunchroom as a noontime aide. I said yes, of course, because I could be near my children and make some extra money in the process. I said God, what was I thinking trying to work two jobs and take care of my children. But I thought to myself, *"Women have been doing this for years, so if they made it, so could I."* I thanked God always for the strength He gave me. This is why I stayed in church around my sisters and brothers in Christ and my pastor. My church family was a part of my strength. They loved on me and me on them, especially some of the sisters I had gotten close with. We became each other's strength, all mothers raising our children and believing in God for better. I wasn't always in my right mind with everything I was dealing with, so being around other women with children and problems was a joy. We figured them out together, us and God.

I stayed in my son's class until school ended and started with the Philadelphia School District the next year. Everything was going as planned. I continued to save money because it was time to move. I had to leave my parent's home; we had truly outgrown our space. The girls were getting antsy with each other, needing their privacy. I started looking and inquiring about some apartments in the area. I needed to be close to both jobs, the kid's school, and close to my parents just in case I needed them.

Working at the school was great; all the kids fell in love with me, Mrs. Hendricks, as I was referred to. My name was called all day in the classroom, hallway, and lunchroom. I even got called during recess or after lunch during their playtime. All the teachers my children had wanted me to volunteer in their classroom to help out, but I couldn't because now it was my job that I was assigned to, not where I wanted, or they wanted me to be.

Soon, I knew why God had me on this journey. There were kids there who needed my mothering, and I gave them what they needed, whether it was food or clothes. I even did some of the little girl's hair in the coat room if they came to school with it undone; I almost lost my job because of it. I prayed over them because of their situation; I even cried some days over them. I felt love for them just like my own. They didn't ask to come into this world and they sure didn't ask to be neglected or mistreated because of their parent's shortcomings. Some of the teachers said don't get too involved with them, but it was hard not to. I knew what my children were dealing with deep down inside, but I couldn't talk about it because they felt a sense of shame. So, the love I had for them was coming from a place that I could relate to. I made it my business to care about these children. I believe that's why God sent me here to be a blessing to some less fortunate child. There were a lot of grandparents raising their grandchildren because some of the children's parents were strung out on drugs, and some had other issues that we could identify with, but nevertheless, why make the children pay for their parent's mistakes? Where I came from, we were a village; we looked out for one another. The neighbor was your neighbor; if a child had to walk to and from school without their parents, other parents stepped in. Unlike today, nobody cares anymore about the children, but I did, and so did my tribe. So, I felt good doing what I was doing for them.

THE SACRIFICE

It was getting close to the holidays and I didn't want to spend another Christmas at my mom's, so I was praying that something would come through. After Thanksgiving, my sister told me that the apartment downstairs from her would be available because the tenants moved out. This would be perfect; I was near all the transportation, the school was within walking distance and my parents' house was too. So I inquired about it, spoke to the landlord and she said I could have it; I couldn't believe it. I felt God's favor all over my life. I felt like He was making a way for me; all I had to do was keep believing.

I was so excited for me and my children. This was my first apartment by myself. I told them the good news. The only thing was that it was so close to the holidays, so I asked them, "Do you want to move now and don't have Christmas or stay at Mom Mom's house and have Christmas?"

They replied, "Let's move, Mom; we would rather be in our own space for the holidays." So we began to pack up our stuff and prepared ourselves to be on our way to our new home.

I got the keys, then went and cleaned up the apartment the way I liked it and started moving stuff in. It was only two bedrooms, but they were nice-sized rooms. The girls shared a room, and my boy stayed back with my parents and came home when he felt like it. I worked diligently to get things in order. I got some guys together and got my furniture out of storage that I paid for 10 times over, but it was mine. I decorated the apartment to my liking. It wasn't long before I turned this apartment into a home. It was a home that my babies could be comfortable in and happy in, and that's all that mattered to me.

I cooked a big dinner for Christmas and my mom had a big surprise for us. The church where my mom served food and always did special things for the neighborhood kids. Even though we didn't live in the neighborhood where the church was, they still honored her wishes. A couple of the guys from the Villanova basketball team came to our apartment to wish us a Merry Christmas and dropped off a few gifts for my children and a basketball for my son; they were ecstatic. They deserved to feel special and my mom made that happen for them. I will be forever grateful to my mom for always being in my corner, even when it was too much.

God was still moving; I got promoted from volunteering in my son's class and a lunchroom aide, now to an SSA Classroom Assistant to the head teacher. Of course, some of the ladies who were there longer than me were upset, but my performance in the class excelled them all. I was glad to have the job, but the only thing that was holding my mind hostage was I couldn't do both jobs, so I had to quit one to be good at the other. I realized that my skill could be used anywhere, so I chose the school district and decided to do hair at the apartment after school hours. This would give me time with my children, so I didn't have to depend on anyone to make sure they got home from school safely, did their homework, had dinner and a bath before bed and, yes, some family time. This made my life easier because I knew what was on my plate, and I did not like the feeling of being overwhelmed. I had to remember the state of mind I was in when I couldn't handle all the stress I was facing, so keeping my mental state together was my first priority, and then making sure my children were OK.

We all had busy lives, dance rehearsals on Mondays, and they were right after school. So we had to rush home, eat, then get on our way. Then there were the school projects, after-school activities, and, let's not talk about Saturday African Cultural Dance for the girls, basketball at the YMCA with my boy, prison on Sunday, and some Saturdays I had to do hair. My life was full; it was a roller coaster ride for me at times. So when I needed to get off the ride, my parents always stepped in and helped me out. I was happy about that. Only when they were home from Jamaica, though, cause they still did their own thing. The retired life was great for them and I loved seeing them be happy.

Well, my children got familiar with the neighborhood and made some new friends and now my house was the house everyone hung out at. It was OK sometimes and other times no, but I didn't like them to go over to other people's houses because I couldn't see what went on in their homes. Furthermore, that's how I grew up; we weren't allowed to be over at other kids' houses. That was a rule in our home growing up and we definitely didn't spend any nights over other kids' homes. So, I was definitely repeating history over here.

Summer is fast approaching and the weather was changing. That meant the kids wanted to hang outside a little longer. I was OK with that, except some of their friends lived in the next block or around the corner and I was leery of that. When I was doing hair, I couldn't keep my eyes on them, so sometimes I said no. Now the girls were getting older, so I got a lot of talk back, lip-smacking, eye-rolling, stumping, and slamming doors. Here we go, now I gotta get in my mama bag and papa bag with some good old fashion punishments and some slammed my door again and watch what happens. My oldest girl is now in high school and was now in the rebellious stage, which drove me bananas. We started bumping heads because she was definitely smelling herself. She was hooking school, not picking up her sister from school, and not coming in on time; man, this girl took me through it.

We became new in the neighborhood, so the girls living around there for a while started bullying my daughter, who was upset about it. So I would say something to them, but they didn't really care about what I was talking about. Soon, they became violent with her, always wanting to fight her, so every other day, it was something. I felt unsafe leaving her home because they always came looking for her; therefore, she had to defend herself. One day after school, I was looking for her because she was so late getting home from school. As I was walking, she was walking towards me and looked distraught.

I asked, "What happened?"

She said, "Some girl came up to me to fight."

I asked, "What happened?"

She said, "I whooped her ass, Mommy; I'm tired of these girls."

I wasn't mad because I endured the same thing growing up. I always had to fight because of my light skin, long hair, and my personality, which these girls didn't like.

I went to the school the next day and had her transferred, thinking that that would be it. Now, the girls in that neighborhood started the same thing. It was not something I looked forward to every other day, but she had to gain her respect. Because some kids don't get it until you handle them and that's just what she did.

I always called my sister for backup because this chick's mother wanted to get involved and I wasn't having it. I called on Jesus, got my bat, and went to help my daughter. It was my job to protect her by all means necessary. This went on for a while; it disturbed my peace and I couldn't find a solution. I couldn't keep her locked in the house, so I had prayer with my prayer partners. I had to seek my God for help.

Things didn't get any better now she wanted to date; this is where the daddy needs to be home. I didn't like any of the boys she chose. They were two or three years older, and they were controlling, but she found it amusing because of her not having her dad around. I was back on another roller coaster ride. I had to think of something quick before the streets won her over. Focusing on my younger kids, I kept my sanity because I knew what the devil was trying to do. I got closer to God and signed my children up with the Big Brother and Sister Program. It was going fine until she got bored. Nothing I did at this point helped.

The situation grew worse, but I couldn't focus on that. I had to keep my house in order. After months of prayer, other violent situations, and many trips to the police station, things were starting to calm down. Now and then, I had to lock her out and not let her back in because she didn't want to follow the rules of my house, so I had to tough-love her.

Time passed, and I went through all these different changes with my girls, but I've never lost hope. I stayed on my knees and in God's face. It wasn't easy, but I wouldn't let the streets have my girls, so I did what I knew best to do my way. After all the drama calmed down and I could trust the girls being home, I signed up for school at night. I wanted to return to school to get my license in management, so I did. My parents helped out, as always. I still did hair in my kitchen and had a nice clientele. They loved coming to get their hair done in my house. We ate and laughed; we made it a whole night in my kitchen. I taught my middle girl how to shampoo hair and braid some of the clients' hair to help me out when I had more than two people waiting to get their hair done. Many clients loved my children; they were always pleasant and well-mannered, a little wild at times, but overall good girls. I told them how to use the stove and oven so they could cook dinner while I attended school at night.

My oldest girl never liked cooking. It reminded me of my sisters coming up; I always cooked in my house because my sister didn't like to and my dad didn't want them to. He loved her and made dinner while my mom was at work. But you best believe they had chores to do every weekend and their reward was renting a few movies and I would let them have a girl sleepover night. I would make popcorn and some Cream of Wheat while we watched movies. I enjoyed my children like my mom enjoyed us growing up. I wanted them to enjoy being kids in the midst of the hardship we were facing. I tried to make it as comfortable as I possibly could. They got an allowance, but they knew it had to be earned by doing their chores.

I couldn't afford to take them on long vacations, so we did day trips with friends or different fun stuff with our church. Sometimes, other family members would take them out for the day, so they never wanted for anything like us when we were growing up. We got everything we needed and some of the stuff we wanted. I wanted my children to see the kind of mother I wanted and needed to be for them because I wanted them to have the same mindset when they get older and have their own children. Nothing in life is free; you must work for what you want.

I made an honest living; I worked two jobs to give my family what they needed. I made sure every holiday was special for them. I did what I could to put a smile on their faces. I worked my jobs to keep a roof over their head, put food on the table, and put clothes on their back so they never had to be jealous of anyone that they thought I had more than them. I told my girls you can have whatever you want in life; you just have to work to get it. The struggle I was in was all about doing right by them. These were life lessons no matter who comes, goes, and stays. This is what you teach your children. I didn't have any men around my children. They didn't have any make-believe uncles.

I understood that this time of being alone wasn't about me feeling or being lonely. It was about me learning how to walk in my singleness while my husband was away to become the woman he was grooming me to be. You see, I never got a chance to live a single life; I went from dating, meeting my husband in high school, having a baby at 19, and then getting married. I was still growing up when I got married; I still had teenage ways. I was forced to grow up because of the choices I made, so I wanted my girls to pay close attention to my life and learn from my experiences. It's all about choices and who and what we connect ourselves to. So here I am, raising three children on my own because of the choices that someone made that took away their rights to be here to help raise them. I had to grow up and take full responsibility for my children, and I had to trust God to help me to do it. God was healing my broken life through this experience and it didn't feel good, but it had to be done for me to become the woman I wanted to be for myself and my children. Especially my girls, they needed this for their journey as well. Our daughters will only know how to become beautiful women by what and how we show them.

I went through my trials now, not caring about what people thought because it was my journey, not theirs. I had God on my side and when things got rough and they do at times, I had my church to go to to release and regroup. My pastor knew that Word and broke it down for us to understand what the Lord was saying to His people. This is what got me through my week.

I continued to raise my children in God's house and they continued to grow. Times were tough for them because they were getting older, attending school dances, graduating, and experiencing life as teenagers. Yes, they missed their father being around, but they too had to adjust. They knew God was with them because I made sure that they understood that. My boy got all settled in with his new basketball team at the YMCA and loved being a part of the Big Brother Program. These things kept my children busy, so they never had time to be depressed. I'm sure they had their personal moments, but they had to keep going just like I did and I encouraged them along the way.

WHERE GOD WANTS ME

My husband's prison time of being up was fast approaching, so I prepared myself and my children. This would be a big change for us. I knew what I had planned and saved for, but I wasn't sure how it would turn out. I became and still was becoming, all I could be in the Lord because I've learned through all that I've been through the good, the bad, and the ugly that everything is a process. We all know that the process is never easy. I knew that I was a different woman now and I had something that I didn't have when he left and that was faith. I didn't have the self-esteem that I have now. I'm a whole different woman; my standards are different. I won't accept certain things or behaviors now. My peace is important to me. There are some things that I won't tolerate anymore, so I knew this would be challenging for both of us. I knew the Lord was on my side, so I wouldn't fail no matter what way it goes. He prepared me for all that I would face. I have help not only from above but from those who love me: my parents, my sisters, those group of women in my church who watched me go through my mess and watched God heal my life and those women who have been through life struggles just as I did. We are never alone in our trials; the devil just wants us to think that we are so we can lose hope.

My journey as a hairstylist wasn't just about doing women's hair but helping other women on their journey called life. Life is full of good and bad; how we go through it makes the difference.

I went on and finished my course at school and got my manager's license. Then, months later, I welcomed my husband home. My children were relieved, not just for him but for me. They watched me do it all by myself with the help of their grandparents, so they understood that we can't do everything by ourselves even though we sometimes have to. They believed in what I taught them about being a team. We can do more together when we work together.

It was just in time for my oldest daughter to go on her prom and graduate from high school, which made her the happiest. It was a journey, but she made it through all the rough times and hard lessons. She understood why I fought so hard for her and her siblings to be great.

I give honor to God, my family, and those church mothers who prayed for us through those rough places. My pastor countless times consoled me and my girls, always ensuring we knew that God and he was on our side. As I grew in my faith, I wanted more for myself and my children. I wanted them to know how to become better, not bitter, in the midst of every storm that may come in their lives. I wanted them to know when you believe in yourself; you can make it. Look to God first and you will come out on the other side. You just have to persevere and keep moving, even when it doesn't look like what you see.

My husband being home was definitely different. He jumped right in and started helping out. He knew what we discussed regarding my business, so we prioritized that first. Looking for a salon wasn't easy, but God already knew where to begin my salon journey. So, after talking to someone, he told me about a salon for rent, so I said, OK, let's go and check it out and to my surprise, it was right down the street from my apartment. So he met with the owners and just like that, we were in. It was already decorated because it was already a salon before, so we moved in and my salon was in the making of becoming something great. Simply Beautiful & Co full-service beauty salon. I hired some young ladies and went on to have a second salon. I worked in both shops until we left the other one. We did great things in the neighborhood; we gave back to the community. I did special events; I did Channel 6 Adopt a Child, where four girls got makeovers for the day as they waited for the families to adopt them. It was great with my mom by my side as my receptionist. She held it down for me while I went back and forth to hair shows and classes to keep up with the latest styles. My salon became really big when I went to a hair show in Atlanta and learned how to do Fusion hair extensions. I returned home and taught it in my shop to my stylist and to others. At $500 ahead, we made that money. We saved up and now it was time for us to leave the apartment.

We bought a house and continued to grow the salon. I never stop grinding in my business. This money we made allowed us to move on to get other businesses started that my husband wanted. I remained in the salon doing what I do best. I ended up leaving my second shop because I needed to be close to home because my oldest had left the nest. It was the two younger ones at home, so I wanted to be closer to them in case of an emergency. So I found one near home, it was perfect. I decorated it how I wanted it with my taste and style, and it was beautiful. We did all kinds of neat stuff there; we had fashion shows and girl's night makeup demos. I was in love with my new place. I stayed there for about five years and then I had to go. Every year, they kept going up on the rent, so I searched for a new home, but I had to put it on pause for a moment because my father took ill.

My mom stopped working at the shop to take care of him. They ended up returning to Jamaica for a while to get him out of the winter weather. They stayed all nine months and I continued to work my business and build up my clientele. I loved my craft. I love getting dressed, putting on makeup, and getting my clients as beautiful as possible. I love making my ladies look good. I practiced good hair care. I always talked about habit and routine because this would give them the beautiful hair and skin they wanted. Beauty was more than skin deep; we had to care for our insides, which was a process for some women. They had to get into the habit of doing something different from what they were taught regarding hair and skin. I was educated in that area; I didn't just do hair; I was a teacher. I had students when I returned to get my manager's license; It was a part of my course teaching how to have beautiful hair and skin. Not just managing a shop, you had to manage how to care for what God gave you as your glory. It was a beautiful cost and would cost you to invest in yourself. Women feel their best when their hair is done and their skin is glowing. So, I was always teaching along with doing my job. It was my pleasure for them to trust me, but there were other times we talked about having faith in God. You know, I heard many stories from my ladies, the things they were going through in their lives. And because of what I went through, I could give them an encouraging word or two.

Now, just because my husband was home didn't mean things were going well because they weren't. I was just in a different place. God had already prepared me for this journey. I didn't know what would happen, but I knew I had God, which was enough for me. He would lead and guide me into all truth. So, I kept it moving because I had a business to grow and two other children to get through school. So, I didn't have time to care about anything else.

My father's illness worsened and my mom had to get him back home.

Once they returned home, he was diagnosed with cancer. This devastated the whole family; I couldn't breathe my whole world was shaken. My mom was a champ; she got him to his treatments every time and made sure he knew that she was his rock. He made it through there for a while.

Later on, I had to have emergency surgery due to some bleeding I had for the past three years. So I was down for a while, and my husband and children cared for me. My mom and dad came over daily to cook, and my father would sit across from my bed and talk to me about life. He let me know that he wasn't going to live long and for me to take care of my mom.

"I know you're not the oldest, but you have weathered some great storms in your life." And he was proud of me for that.

He gave me his blessings, which was hard for him because my dad wasn't affectionate. He was a man with three girls that he loved but didn't always show it emotionally.

After some time passed, my dad got worse. He ended up back in the hospital for 71 days. We spent Christmas with him. After my surgery, I wasn't in the best shape, but I saw my father in the hospital. At Christmas and New Year's 2010, my father came home on January 3rd and I went and spent the whole night with him. I was praying, singing a song and reading to him; he was OK with that. He told me to be all that I can be, continue doing my business and keep believing in God. I knew then, just looking at my father, that it wouldn't be long.

I prayed silently to God and he said, "Winnie, I hear you praying."

"Daddy, I really thought you were sleeping."

He said, "I can hear you in my sleep."

It was getting late, and I needed to get home and get some rest. I wasn't back in the salon because I was still healing from my surgery. However, other stylists were still working and holding it down while I was out. I went home and went to bed and I just couldn't sleep. I thought I was dreaming; I heard a strong wind and some heavy feet stomping through the streets. So I woke up, looked out my window and it was something I'd never seen before.

I can't even describe it, but I remember saying, *"What the hell is that?"*

My husband nudged me and said, "Are you OK?"

I said, "I guess I was dreaming."

I looked at my clock, and it was 6 a.m., and my phone rang. It was my nephew and I heard my mom screaming in the background. I jumped up, got my shoes and clothes on and my husband ran behind me. We got to my mom's and the ambulance was in front of our door.

I jumped out of the car, ran into the house, and held my mom and she said, "He's gone."

I yelled, "No Mommy!"

They wouldn't let us up the stairs while still working on him. So, I continued to comfort my mother until we could go upstairs to see my dad. My sisters came, other neighbors came over, and my sister called his family and they came over. Finally, they came downstairs and told us that he was gone. I couldn't believe my daddy was gone; the only man who really loved me was now gone. I thought to myself, *"How was my mother or I going to make it without him."* This was the hardest thing I ever had to deal with, but I remember God will comfort me through my other trials. I called on Him to help me and my family get through this time. And he did; it wasn't easy. We buried my father and went on with our lives; it wasn't easy. I have my mom on my prayer list because I knew she wouldn't be OK for a while.

I returned to work, and my clients and church family were very supportive during that time. My pastor did the eulogy and it was great. My family will forever have a hole in our hearts. Especially me, my dad was everything my children needed when my husband went to prison. He cared for us; he took my son under his wings so he would know how to become a man. This was hard, but I held onto the words that he spoke to me and I ran with them. I saw him two more times in my dreams, letting me know that he was OK. Nothing else to lose, everything to gain; that was my mindset. I knew I had to step it up for my family. It's always one in the family that everyone looks to to hold the family together and that was me. I didn't ask for this position; it just fell on me.

FINDING MY WAY

So here we are on another assignment. I prayed more now than ever. My mom needed us and our children knew that we had to keep mom mom close; that's what my father would have wanted.

My boy was getting ready to graduate high school. Look how far we have come. Time waits for no one. We all were encouraged to be all that we could be. That's what my father said to all his grandchildren and my children did just that. After her long journey to finding herself, my oldest girl went to college and graduated with honors. My middle child stayed at the shop with me. I knew my dad would have been proud and we know he is smiling down on us.

Our business and now in another financial bracket; we bought a home in another state. It belonged to one of the Eagles players; he wanted a bigger home for him and his family and God allowed us to get it. We were now on the other side of the fence, a life we could never imagine living. This house was immaculate. It had a pool big enough for at least 10 or more, a Jacuzzi, and a hot tub all outside. This home was beautiful. I had my own walk-in closet, five bedrooms, and a finished basement with a bar. We put a pool table and all the games downstairs for entertainment, an office, living room, dining room, and lounge. We furnished every part of the house. We had weekend gatherings, pool parties, comedy shows, and cookouts. When our guests came over, they couldn't believe how we came up from where we started. Nobody but God. We christened our home, had a housewarming where we asked all of our guest to wear white, we invited our families and friends. My husband was happy, so was I. My middle child got married at our home. My husband insisted that she get married in this home. He was excited to give her away; after not being around to see them grow up, he wanted to go all out for them. He spent $75,000 on this wedding. He bought my son a 2010 Camero for his graduation and gave my oldest her own business to run. God had truly blessed us. Living the good life had its perks but it came with some things that didn't agree with my spirit. My marriage was starting to change; things started happening that shouldn't have never been happening. Certain behaviors started appearing, late nights got later, phone calls and text messages went on after hours, rumors started surfacing, and my happy home wasn't happy anymore. I complained about it, started worrying, lost my hair, and gained a whole lot of weight; I started feeling ugly again. It didn't matter how pretty I looked on the outside; I was torn up on the inside like I felt before and I couldn't shake it. I confronted him numerous times, but it was always denial, it wasn't him or I was imagining things. So I went to my pastor and he suggested counseling for us. So we went for all that it was worth, and there were promises made and that he wasn't doing anything wrong, but that's not what I was feeling. I went to work every day with tears in my eyes, my pride hurt, and I felt like 10 fools and a mule because I waited 10 years for this man; I built a home, raised our children in the fear of God, and kept myself for only him and this is what I get. Now, I was hurt, but it didn't stop me from going to church. I'll go with pain in my heart after being up all night cussing and fussing about where he had been at half the night. I would look like hell and it showed in my personality. Thank God I had some sisters that held me up. Of course, I cried to some of my close friends who happened to be my clients, and they couldn't believe it because they watched me go through this hell and come out with my head held high, even if it hurt to keep it up. "How dare him," they said.

After months and months of this drama, I finally left my dream home and moved back into my house. I couldn't let this thing tear me down; it took so long to get here. I couldn't let this steal my joy and peace or make me become the woman that I used to be. So I started encouraging myself through God's Word and stayed around other women who went through the same stuff; we encouraged each other. I returned to the position God had me in while he was away. We stayed together, but a part. I couldn't lower my standards for some stuff. Material things don't make you happy if the person does not bring you peace. We agreed to remain married but separated.

We managed our businesses. I needed to move my shop, so we found a building that would be perfect, so we bought it. It had a second floor, which we rented once everything was done. We gutted out the whole first floor, remodeled it and turned it into a beautiful salon with six chairs for some new stylists. Simply Beautiful had a new home. I made a safe and relaxing environment for my current and new clients to come and enjoy the comfort of being in my place of business. Everyone who came through those doors felt the presence of God because even though I was going through my stuff, I still kept my head up, smiled, and looked pretty. I had faith that God was going to fix this, too. I had to be patient, but while waiting, I stayed in my prayer position, continued my spiritual journey with the Lord and shared it along the way. This journey that I was on just wasn't about doing hair. It was about healing other women just like me. Through all the stuff I endured, God had to show me that beauty is only skin deep; it's the inner beauty that makes us beautiful. My journey as a hairstylist was about helping those women that I came in contact with to know their worth and to believe in themselves. No matter what, speak life in every dead place in your life and set some boundaries. Healing from the inside takes time.

Make time for yourself because you are important. God has plans for us women, but we must be healed, whole, and fit for the Master's use. So you can't just look good on the outside; you have to feel good on the inside. That's why I could talk to my clients about my situation because I knew what God did for me. All ages of women would come into my salon and compliment me on how good I looked, how beautiful my children were, and how nice my salon was, but they didn't know what it took to get here. God kept me just for another woman. Who is God keeping you for?

I went through my trials with my husband and decided he wasn't the man for me, so we decided to go on different paths. I wasn't the same woman that he left 10 years ago. I grew up I had different values and standards. I wasn't perfect by no means, but I knew what I wanted in a man and I knew what I didn't want. I knew what I deserved and what I didn't deserve. I finally was OK with walking alone. We were two different people now; we still kept it together for our children, but that's it. God prepared me for this, and even though it hurt, I knew I would be fine while I was in His care. I stood on His word concerning my life. I knew it would be challenging through the years, but I had faith in my God, who never failed me.

My family continued to grow; I became a grandmom 10 times over. My business grew and I continued to make women beautiful inside and out. I spoke life to them, listened to their stories, heard their hearts crying, felt their pain, and reassured them that they were still beautiful and that real beauty takes time. I did all this while I was still hurting. I never wanted my marriage to end; I believed in love and happy endings. Even though I had faith in my God, there were times that I thought He failed me; I thought this was all for nothing, but I had to stop doubting and start back believing.

My knees were burning because I cried over and over again, asking God why. Why am I here again? Life is about choices and sometimes the choices we make aren't always best for us. So, our suffering may not be a result from what we did wrong; it could be from the people we choose to connect ourselves to. Connection can cause a disconnect from what we've been taught to do or not to do. But God put all things in their proper place.

TAKE FLIGHT

Now a hairstylist for over 32 years, I have had the privilege of not only making women look beautiful but making them feel it as well.

My saying in my salon is, "If you can imagine it, then you can become it." As I journey in this business called a hairstylist, I've learned that we are way more than that; we are a hairapist short for the term therapist. We hear all the stories and all the secrets. We laugh, cry, fuss, and cuss, but it's all in love because all women need an outlet to let their hair down. My place is for all women of all ages to come in and experience the love God gave me for other women. What a blessing!

Now, me and my old clients that been with me from the beginning always have a spot, even if it's just to laugh and chat about the old times in my kitchen, doing their hair late at night, eating, talking to the kids, getting hair ready for church on Sunday. Sometimes, we pray, get the children together in the house and pray for them. These things got us through our trials, being there for one another. Maturing in God wasn't about just me, but the many women who will come after me that I showed the way. I was glad that I shared that beauty with my clients. I pray daily for other women to manifest in my life as I did. Now, I pray the same prayer for every woman I encounter in my shop or on the streets. And through my prayers, I'm reminded of those women I encountered earlier in my journey who didn't wear makeup or jewelry and only wore dresses because of their faith was in God. The Word of God says in 1 Peter 3:3-4 (NIV), *"Your beauty should not come from outward adornment, such as elaborate hairstyles and the wearing of gold jewelry or fine clothes. Rather, it should be that of your inner self, the unfading beauty of a gentle and quiet spirit, which is of great worth in God's sight."* I now understand what real beauty is and how to walk in it.

All the things I suffered from the real Woman of God called me to come through that. It made me feel good that I didn't give up, no matter how hard it got. I found out that beautifulness takes time. I told my clients to change how they think about themselves and be patient with yourself while you're going through your trials. Forgive yourself and all your mistakes, and ask God to forgive your sins, shortcomings, and private struggles. This is between you and Him, and don't ever trade your uniqueness to be what you admire in someone else. Stay who you are; love who you are; fix your own crown first. God created us with a purpose that only you can fulfill. Be happy, no matter what you face in life, keep a positive outlook on things. Stay away from anything and anyone that doesn't speak life. These are the few principles I use to help me become that beautiful woman inside first, then out. I called it my recipe for beauty and becoming a successful woman. It takes time. The Bible says in Philippians 4: 6-7, *"Be anxious for nothing, but in everything by prayer and supplication with thanksgiving, let your request be made known to God and the peace of God, which suppresses all understanding will guard your hearts and minds through Christ Jesus. Be patient with yourself while you're doing what's right in the sight of God."* The first thing I had to do was believe in myself and that God would come through for me. Even when it didn't look like it, I stood on the Word of God concerning faith. Hebrews 11:1, *"Now faith is the substance of things hoped for the evidence of things not seen."* God wanted me to trust Him even if I didn't see what He promised.

The second thing that added to my life was confidence. Get your confidence up. I was always confident when I did hair because I knew what I was doing. I practiced all my hairdos and I taught myself how to do a lot of the hairstyles just by doing them, looking at a magazine or a video. But having confidence in myself was hard. Philippians 1:6 says, *"Being confident of this very thing that he which has begun a good work in you will perform it until the day of Christ."* That means He will finish what He started; just keep believing that He can and He will. If you want to go to college, go. If you want to take a trade, take it. If you want to get married, do it. But whatever you decide to do, do it with confidence and be OK with your decision. Hold your head high in anything you choose to do that is positive; that speaks volumes.

Next, stay focused and concentrate on your goals, which are important to your success. Don't get distracted by things or people that don't pertain to your goals. So many people start stuff and don't finish because they get distracted easily. That was me until I realized the devil kept me from reaching my goals.

Next, be consistent. Consistency is the vehicle to get you to your destination. You can't arrive on time without it. Nothing will happen in our lives in the time frame that God wants us to if we don't stay consistent. I found that one of the most frustrating things in a relationship is when there's no consistency. It will suffer if you're not consistent in treating your wife right in your marriage. If you're not consistent with paying your bills on time, it messes up your credit. I can go on and on about consistency, but let's move on.

We must stay our course if we want to see change and when you feel yourself getting off track, just slide back on track and you will be fine. Just apply the principles; faith is the main ingredient. You have to remember I said that first. Things don't always look like what we want them to and here is where you need to keep it together. Because through all the challenges you will face, I don't want you to leave this one thing out. That's why I'm saying it again. Faith is the substance of things hoped for and evidence of things not seen. So even when you believe, have confidence, and even stay focused, or you may have stayed consistent, things can look like they are not moving along or going the way we think they should go. It will be our faith that pushes that thing through. Speak life, even when it's hard to do. God sees that as us having faith that He will come through no matter what we see or don't see.

I was very attentive to the tasks I was given, especially my children and my business. It was not always in my marriage because I felt I was in it by myself. You can't be married to yourself, to be fooled by that saying I married myself; let me know how that works. But I stayed attentive to everything God had given me to watch over or even as an assignment because I knew the reward was great. So I made sure that I kept my head in the game because of that alone. It was hard at times, but I couldn't drop the ball; too much was at stake. So I prayed this 2 Peter 1:5-9 (NIV) *"For this very reason, make every effort to add to your faith, goodness and to goodness, knowledge and to knowledge, self-control and to self-control, perseverance and to perseverance, godliness and to godliness, mutual affection and to mutual affection, love for if you possess these qualities and increasing measure, they will keep you from being ineffective and productive in your knowledge of our Lord Jesus, but whoever does not have them is nearsighted and blind, forgetting that they have been cleansed from their past sin."*

Don't get caught up. Remember where you came from and how long it took to learn from your mistakes. Remember how long it took for you to get here, where you are right now in your life. Don't let anything keep you from getting your reward that awaits you. Be good to yourself and others; it's all a part of being the beautiful, spirit-filled woman that God created you to be. You have already been through the fire. You identified your failures and shortcomings. You already suffered some losses and you and only you know what it took for you to get to this place in your life.

And finally, be vigilant. I don't care who you have to push aside. I don't care whose feelings you have to hurt. Don't allow anyone to stop you or hold you back from becoming a better you. You will look back and thank God for allowing you to live through this. I thank God that I leaned on Him to take me through the valley. I thank God for allowing me another and another chance to get it right. He gave me courage, strength and the tenacity to go on, even when I had to do it by myself. We are never alone with Him; I dedicate my life changes to my daughters to show them what real beauty looks like. It's successful in all God's glory and it didn't happen overnight; it happened over time. That's what beautiful, seasoned women look like from inside and out.

Over time, keep your confidence up. Stay in tune with God, spiritually, emotionally and physically, if you know what I mean. Remember, you are a daughter of the most high God and this is what He says about His daughters in Proverbs 31:29-31 (KJV) *"Many daughters have done virtuously, but thou excellest them all favour is deceitful, and beauty is vain:*

But a woman that feareth the Lord, she shall be praised. Give her the fruit of her hands and let her own works praise her in the gates. "

I now have a platform to provide healing inside and out. God gave me that platform through my business, Simply Beautiful, so that I can show women how to be beautiful inside and then out. So that the essence of her beauty can follow her wherever she goes, on her job, for the women she may encounter on the streets, that essence will follow her, no matter where she finds herself in life.

Thank you for reading my journey to this place called beautiful. I hope it blessed your life.

ABOUT THE AUTHOR

Rosalyn A. Gillis, a distinguished 57-year-old African-American woman, hails from the vibrant city of Philadelphia, Pennsylvania, where her journey of inspiration and resilience began. She is the embodiment of a rich and storied heritage, born to the late and great Hayward Gillis Jr. and the indomitable Carolyn L. Gillis, both of whom were steeped in the traditions and culture of the American South. It is from this deep wellspring of Southern roots that Rosalyn draws her captivating Southern flavor, infusing her life's narrative with a unique and intriguing charm that pervades her work and the compelling story she has to tell.

"The Making Of A Beautiful Woman LLC" serves as my dedicated platform, a sanctuary for women of all ages who have weathered life's most arduous storms and may have momentarily lost their connection to the beautiful spirits residing within them. This endeavor is a profound journey of healing, meticulously crafted to rekindle the inner flame that adversity may have momentarily dimmed. 'The Making of Beautiful'· represents a heartfelt odyssey towards renewed self-discovery, empowerment, and the reawakening of the resilient and radiant woman that resides within every soul. Join me on this transformative path as we unveil the beauty that exists both inside and out."

"The Making of a Beautiful Woman was born from the heart of my two-decade journey as the proud owner of 'Simply Beautiful and Company,'· a haven of beauty and transformation. Over 32 remarkable years, I have had the immense privilege of serving countless women, not merely by enhancing their external beauty but by kindling the radiance of their inner spirits. Within the walls of my salon, a powerful mantra echoes: 'if you can imagine it, you can become it.' I firmly believe that my calling from a higher power is to inspire women to transcend the boundaries of superficial beauty and embark on a profound voyage to become the best versions of themselves. The truth is, beautiful women aren't crafted overnight; they are masterpieces crafted over time. Join me on this remarkable journey to unveil the essence of true beauty, one that emanates from the inside out."

www.ingramcontent.com/pod-product-compliance
Lightning Source LLC
Chambersburg PA
CBHW051215120626
46547CB00013B/1370